The Los Alamos Primer

Robert Serber

The Los Alamos Primer

The First Lectures on How To
Build An Atomic Bomb

Annotated by Robert Serber

Edited with an Introduction by
Richard Rhodes

UNIVERSITY OF CALIFORNIA PRESS

Berkeley / Los Angeles / London

University of California Press
Berkeley and Los Angeles, California

University of California Press
London, England

Copyright © 1992 by Robert Serber

Library of Congress Cataloging-in-Publication Data

Serber, R. (Robert)
  The Los Alamos primer : The first lectures on how to build an
atomic bomb / Robert Serber: annotated by Robert Serber;
edited by Richard Rhodes.
      p. cm.
  Based on a set of 5 lectures given by R. Serber during the first
two weeks of April 1943 as an indoctrination course in
connection with the starting of the Los Alamos Project.
  Includes bibliographical references and index.
  ISBN 978-0-520-07576-4
  1. Atomic bomb—United States—History. 2. Manhattan
Project (U.S.)—History. 3. Los Alamos Scientific Laboratory—
History. 4. Physicists—Biography. I. Rhodes, Richard. II. Title.
QC773.A1S47   1992
623.4'5119—dc20   91–14068
                                                          CIP

Printed in the United States of America

17 16 15 14 13 12 11 10 09 08
18 17 16 15 14 13 12 11

The paper used in this publication meets the minimum
requirements of ANSI/NISO Z39.48-1992 (R 1997)
(*Permanence of Paper*). ∞

Contents

Richard Rhodes:
Introduction

In late March 1943, in a dark time of world war, young scientists began arriving in Santa Fe, New Mexico, prepared to work on a new secret-weapons project just getting under way nearby. Officially they had been informed only that the project's successful culmination would probably end the war. Unofficially they understood that the work for which they were volunteering to live behind barbed wire for years to come, to return home only in cases of dire emergency, to delay finishing their doctoral studies or beginning their careers, was unprecedented and millennial; unofficially they whispered that they had signed on to attempt nothing less than inventing, designing, assembling, and testing the world's first atomic bombs—releasing explosively for the first time the enormous energy confined within the nuclei of atoms. Other secret installations around the United States employing tens of thousands of workers—at Oak Ridge, Tennessee; in Chicago at the University; on a barren site beside the Columbia River at Hanford, Washington—would painstakingly accumulate the few kilograms of exotic metals that the weapons would require; but the eager young team at Los Alamos would construct the actual weapons themselves.

Signing on to invent and craft new weapons of unprecedented destructiveness may seem bloodthirsty from today's long perspective of limited war and nuclear truce. Those were different times. War was general throughout the world, a pandemic of manmade death. Hundreds of thousands of other Americans—siblings and classmates and friends—were risking their lives on the front lines of North Africa and the Pacific islands. The death toll had already accumulated into the millions. There was reason to believe that the Germans might be at work on an atomic bomb, might even be ahead in the race, and the prospect of a Third Reich victorious with nuclear weapons chilled the soul. A new weapon in the American arsenal so destructive that it might frighten the belligerents into surrender seemed to many, in Winston Churchill's postwar phrase, "a miracle of deliverance."

The Army loaded the volunteers into olive-drab staff cars and jitneys and hauled them northwest of the New Mexico capital into the desert country beyond the Rio Grande. The vehicles negotiated a vertiginous unbarricaded road up the sheer wall of a canyon and came out onto a high, pine-forested plateau that jutted from the collapsed cone of the largest extinct volcano in the world. Los Alamos, the mesa was called, named for the cottonwoods that grew in the steep canyons that guarded its fastness. The construction site at the west end of the plateau, where a secret laboratory was being built, was a mess—heavy trucks and graders mucking through spring mud—but a core of handsome chinked-log buildings left over from the boys' school that had formerly occupied the site offered sanctuary.

There was no time to waste. If the project on the Hill, as the place came to be called, would in fact end the war, then its challenges would be measured in human lives. While construction proceeded—wooden laboratories like stretched army barracks going up south of the school buildings across the main road, long vacuum tanks and massive electromagnets arriving shrouded on laboring flatbed trucks—discussion at least could begin. It would continue, unceasing and obsessive, for two and a half years, to culminate in a vast, blinding fireball that turned a cold desert night into day.

The several dozen young Americans—graduate students and recent postdocs—who came to Los Alamos found themselves working with distinguished men of science whom many of them knew only from their textbooks: J. Robert Oppenheimer, the secret laboratory's new director, a wealthy, cosmopolitan New Yorker who had come back from study in Europe in the late 1920s to found the first great American school of theoretical physics at the University of California at Berkeley; Enrico Fermi, the Italian Nobel laureate, one of the three or four greatest physicists of the century; I. I. Rabi, an American Nobel laureate, small and witty, who visited the Hill as a consultant but devoted his primary energies to working on radar at MIT; Edward Teller, a deep-voiced, excitable Hungarian theoretician of great versatility; Hans Bethe, an emigré from the anti-Semitic persecutions of Nazi Germany who had puzzled out the chain of nuclear reactions that fires the stars. Despite this leavening of older men (Oppenheimer was thirty-eight), the group's average age was only twenty-four.

An Oppenheimer protégé, Robert Serber, a slim young Berkeley theoretician, quiet and shy but very much in command of his subject, began the work of the new secret laboratory with a series of lectures. Serber had guided a secret seminar at Berkeley the previous summer that invented and explored the ideas he was about to discuss; Oppenheimer, Bethe, and Teller were among the participants at the summer meetings in the conference room of Oppenheimer's Berkeley office. Now at Los Alamos, with chalk in hand and a blackboard set up behind him, Serber proceeded to open the door to a new world.

"The object of the project," the young theoretician began, scanning the expectant faces, "is to produce a *practical military weapon* in the form of a bomb in which the energy is released by a fast neutron chain reaction in one or more of the materials known to show nuclear fission." That was news as well as confirmation, and his listeners let out their breaths. Those who had worked on the secret project elsewhere were amazed and delighted. Previously, to preserve military secrecy, they had only been allowed to know what immediately affected their work; now, as Oppenheimer had promised when he invited them to work at Los Alamos, they would know all. The barbed wire that would fence them in, the travel restrictions that would confine them there in the middle of the wilderness for the duration of the war, would also allow them scientific freedom of speech. Oppenheimer had convinced the army that open discussion, the lifeblood of science, was the only way to get the job done.

Bob Serber delivered five lectures in all. The raw new library rang with debate. Crew-cut Edward Condon, the associate director of the secret laboratory, kept notes. From day to day Condon and Serber worked up the notes into twenty-four mimeographed pages dense with formulas, graphs, and crude drawings — the essence of what anyone in the world knew at that point about a secret new technology that would change forever the way nations thought about war. Puckishly, the two physicists titled the document the *Los Alamos Primer*. New recruits would be handed a copy as they arrived on the Hill (and arrive they did in the months to come, the Hill population doubling every nine months until it numbered more than five thousand by August 1945, the end of the war).

The *Primer* and the Frisch-Peierls memorandum of early 1940 (included here as an appendix) carry a greater freight of historic import than perhaps any other documents in the history of technology. Neither document is a recipe for building an atomic bomb. The *Primer* corresponds in this regard to Henry DeWolf Smythe's 1945 book *Atomic Energy for Military Purposes*, published officially by the United States government at the time the atomic bombing of Japan was announced, which describes at a similar level of generality the effort of physics and engineering that developing the first atomic bombs required.

There was never in any case any scientific "secret" to the atomic bomb, except the crucial secret, revealed at Hiroshima and Nagasaki, that such a weapon would work.[1] The discovery that led directly to the bomb was the achievement of an Austrian physicist and two German chemists—Lise Meitner, Otto Hahn, and Fritz Strassmann. It came as a complete surprise during the 1938 Christmas season, nine months before the beginning in Europe of the Second World War, culminating three years of experiments. The previous summer Meitner, of Jewish antecedents, had escaped Nazi Germany for Sweden, but Hahn and Strassmann in Berlin turned to her for interpretation when their experiments bombarding uranium nitrate with low-energy neutrons produced barium as a product, rather than the radium they expected to find.

Meitner pondered this odd result during the Christmas holiday while visiting friends in the village of Kungälf in western Sweden with her young physicist nephew Otto Robert Frisch, trying to imagine a mechanism that might account for it. Hahn and Strassmann deduced that they had somehow burst the uranium nucleus into two more or less equal fragments, one of which was barium. Previous probings of the nucleus had always demonstrated a clear relationship between energy in and energy out—a lower-energy particle chipping only a small piece off the nucleus, a higher-energy particle chipping proportionately more. To explain this anomalous new reaction, Meitner and Frisch had to visualize the nucleus differently. They were used to thinking of it as rigid and hard. Within the past two years, however, the Danish physicist Niels Bohr, with whom Frisch worked, had developed a model of the nucleus that treated it as if it were a liquid drop, wobbly and soft. Under certain conditions, Meitner and Frisch

1. There were engineering and industrial secrets, of course—how to manufacture filters that would efficiently separate U^{235} from U^{238}, for example; how to separate plutonium chemically from irradiated uranium; how to compose and shape explosive lenses—and these secrets continue quite properly to be protected.

realized, neutron bombardment might indeed disturb such an unstable nucleus to the point where it divided and reformed into two or more smaller drops. They reasoned that such a division and more compact rearrangement should result in the conversion of a small fraction of the mass of the nucleus—equal to about one-fifth of the mass of a proton—into energy. That outcome was unprecedented and extraordinary. The most energetic chemical reactions—burning hydrogen with oxygen, for example—release about 5 electron volts per atom. Meitner calculated, and Frisch soon demonstrated by experiment, that a neutron moving at energies of only a few electron volts, bombarding an atom of uranium and bursting it, would release about 170 million electron volts per atom. The newly discovered reaction was ferociously exothermic, output exceeding input by at least five orders of magnitude. Here was a new source of energy like nothing seen before in all the long history of the world.

Back in Copenhagen, where he worked at Bohr's institute, Frisch conferred with Meitner in Stockholm by telephone early in the new year to agree on a name for the new reaction; thinking of the liquid-drop model of the nucleus and borrowing from biology the term for cell division, they named it nuclear fission.

Early in January 1939 Hahn and Strassmann published their results in the German scientific journal *Naturwissenschaften*. Meitner and Frisch followed up with letters to the British journal *Nature*. Within a year more than one hundred papers had appeared on the new reaction, reporting work by physicists throughout the world.

It was immediately evident to physicists everywhere that nuclear fission might serve as the basis for new sources of power and new weapons of war. Work on military applications began first in Germany, where the Reich Ministry of Education convened a secret conference on April 29, 1939, that led to a research program and a ban on uranium exports. Independently during the same month, a Japanese army general ordered military applications explored. In the United States, Hungarian emigré physicists Leo Szilard, Edward Teller, and Eugene Wigner communicated their concerns about German developments to President Franklin D. Roosevelt through a letter from Albert Einstein that Roosevelt reviewed on October 11, 1939. The British took a first look in 1939, stalled, and then, catalyzed by a memorandum from the physicists Otto Robert Frisch and Rudolf Peierls, emigrés from Nazi Germany resident in Birmingham, began again in earnest early in 1940. The Soviet physicist Igor Kurchatov alerted his government to the possible military significance of nuclear fission in 1939. The German invasion of the USSR in June 1941 delayed Soviet research toward an atomic bomb, but a modest research program began in Moscow in early 1943.

Late in 1941, with the British cooperating, the United States expanded its effort to an all-out, multimillion-dollar program. By 1943, reflecting that commitment, the Manhattan Project had achieved the first manmade nuclear reaction, Fermi's famous "pile" of graphite and natural uranium assembled in a doubles squash court under the stands of Stagg Field on the campus of the University of Chicago. It had begun building factories for creating kilogram quantities of the new manmade element plutonium and separating rare fissile uranium—the isotope U^{235}—from ordinary uranium that by 1945 would rival in scale and in value of investment the contemporary U.S. automobile industry. Japanese efforts never advanced beyond the laboratory. The German program lost priority in 1942 to more immediately promising military research.

The crew at Los Alamos had its work cut out for it. It needed to learn more about the physics of fast-neutron fission, in particular the many nuclear cross sections that could only be ascertained by experiment. It needed to determine the critical masses of uranium and plutonium in various configurations and to approach a fast-neutron chain reaction as closely as possible in the laboratory without blowing up the Hill. The metallurgy of uranium and plutonium was largely unknown and had to be mastered. Some sort of device had to be invented that would nestle inertly among the pieces of nuclear material in a bomb but release a burst of neutrons on cue to start the bomb's chain reaction when those pieces came together. Hardly anyone on the Hill knew anything about explosives, but before the work was done they would invent a new technology that treated explosives as precision instruments and would machine some twenty thousand cast blocks of high explosives into precise shapes as if they were merely blocks of metal. Radiation medicine was another serious concern; the effects of whole-body radiation on human beings were largely unknown. Bombers would have to be found large enough to carry weapons that might measure ten feet in length and weigh ten thousand pounds, their bomb bays modified accordingly and their crews trained. Whether the mechanism that assembled a critical mass would be a gun or something more exotic, the bombs would require suitable armored ballistic casings to shape their fall through the air. The bombs would need reliable sensors to set them off at a preset altitude above their targets.

Central to all this activity at Los Alamos was the problem of designing a weapon that would safely transport one or more critical masses of nuclear material—uranium or plutonium—to target and then assemble them reliably at the precise moment required. Where U^{235} was concerned, solving that problem proved to be straightforward. One of the two weapons ultimately delivered to the Pacific for use against the Japanese—Little Boy, it was called—was a gun design that incorporated about 50 kilograms of highly purified U^{235}. Those three critical masses were distributed between a ring fixed around the muzzle of a small cannon and a "bullet" inserted into the cannon breech ahead of bags of cordite, to be fired at the appropriate time up the barrel to complete the supercritical assembly. Los Alamos considered the Little Boy design sufficiently conservative that it delivered the weapon without proof testing; Little Boy was one of a kind.

Because plutonium is more highly radioactive than uranium, however, it was clear from the beginning that trying to explode plutonium efficiently using a gun mechanism would push the limits of artillery technology. No other straightforward method of assembly presented itself, and work on a plutonium gun went ahead at Los Alamos until the summer of 1944. At that time the first reactor-bred Pu^{239} arrived from Oak Ridge. When the Italian physicist Emilio Segré measured the nuclear characteristics of the reactor-bred plutonium, he found its rate of spontaneous fission unacceptably high; it was contaminated with a significant, inseparable admixture of Pu^{240}. Segré's measurements indicated that even in a cannon capable of attaining a muzzle velocity of three thousand feet per second, the plutonium would predetonate, melting the bullet and target ring before the parts had time to join to produce a high-yield explosion.

That realization brought Los Alamos to crisis. Despite the vast scale of the separation plants the Manhattan Project was constructing, separating U^{235} from U^{238} was so difficult a physical process that the United States expected to accumulate no more than one bomb's worth of the fissile uranium isotope by the summer of 1945. Without plutonium, that is, a secret weapons project in which the U.S. government was investing more than two billion dollars and which had higher priority than any other program of the war would result at best in only one bomb. And no one believed that one bomb, however destructive, could make a decisive difference in the course of the war.

Oppenheimer conferred with his colleagues and his superiors about the plutonium crisis and decided to attempt to develop a wholly new technology for assembling a critical mass. David Hawkins's technical history of Los Alamos notes that implosion, as the new technology was called, was "the only real hope [at that point], and from current evidence not a very good one."[2]

A volume of fissionable material becomes critical—begins to explode—when a sufficient mass is assembled in a shape that allows a chain reaction to proceed. A solid sphere of 5 kilograms of Pu^{239} surrounded by a thick shield (called a "tamper") will explode immediately upon assembly; the same tamped 5 kilograms formed into a hollow shell is safely subcritical. Through the autumn and winter of 1944 and into the spring of 1945, the men and women on the Hill worked night and day to find a way to use explosives to squeeze hollow shells of plutonium rapidly into solid spheres. Theoreticians covered blackboards with calculations; explosions clattered from the canyons. The changing geometry was difficult to calculate by hand in a reasonable period of time in those days before digital computers, and tests were marred by troublesome detonation-wave intersections that caused jets and spalling. Shells got thicker and smaller as designs got more conservative.

John von Neumann, a brilliant Hungarian mathematician who visited Los Alamos from time to time as a consultant, contributed a crucial breakthrough. Von Neumann designed an intricate spherical assembly of blocks of high explosives that formed an explosive lens, redirecting spherical shock waves expanding from multiple points of detonation into a single, uniformly spherical shock wave converging on a nuclear core. Edward Teller contributed a further breakthrough, the knowledge that given sufficient pressure, even solid metal can be significantly compressed. Instead of trying to crumple thin-walled shells into solid spheres, the physicists working on implosion came to understand, they could squeeze a thick-walled, nearly solid sphere of plutonium to greater density, bringing its atoms closer together and thereby making a subcritical mass supercritical. "The immediate and obvious advantage of implosion," writes the physicist Luis W. Alvarez, who worked on it at Los Alamos, "is that the material 'assembles' so

2. David Hawkins, *Manhattan District History, Project Y, The Los Alamos Project*, v. I (Los Alamos Scientific Laboratory, 1947), 82.

quickly under the pressure of the high-speed shock wave that it doesn't have time to predetonate."[3]

The device tested at Trinity Site in the New Mexico desert at 5:30 A.M. on July 16, 1945, was an implosion mechanism with a plutonium core. It exploded with a force equivalent to 18,600 tons of TNT, the first full-scale nuclear explosion on earth. I. I. Rabi watched it from a base camp some ten miles away:

> We were lying there, very tense, in the early dawn, and there were just a few streaks of gold in the east; you could see your neighbor very dimly. Those ten seconds were the longest ten seconds that I ever experienced. Suddenly, there was an enormous flash of light, the brightest light I have ever seen or that I think anyone has ever seen. It blasted; it pounced; it bored its way right through you. It was a vision which was seen with more than the eye. It was seen to last forever. You would wish it would stop; altogether it lasted about two seconds. Finally it was over, diminishing, and we looked toward the place where the bomb had been; there was an enormous ball of fire which grew and grew and it rolled as it grew; it went up into the air, in yellow flashes and into scarlet and green. It looked menacing. It seemed to come toward one.
>
> A new thing had just been born; a new control; a new understanding of man, which man had acquired over nature.[4]

Little Boy was loading for shipment from San Francisco on the heavy cruiser *Indianapolis* at the time of the test; three high-explosive preassemblies for the implosion bomb, nicknamed Fat Man, would follow along by air soon after.

In those last months of the war only a few questioned if the formidable new weapons should be used. Most found better reasons to use them than not. Germany had surrendered, but the United States was preparing to invade Japan. President Harry S Truman's military advisers expected the invasion to exact a toll of tens of thousands of American and hundreds of thousands of Japanese lives, a loss the new weapons might forestall if they proved to be decisive.

The Soviet Union, which had not yet declared war on Japan, had pledged to do so on August 15; if atomic bombs forced a Japanese

3. Luis W. Alvarez, *Alvarez* (Basic Books, 1987), 131. Alvarez himself contributed a further crucial invention, a method of detonating the shell of high explosive blocks surrounding the plutonium core simultaneously from thirty-two points spaced equally around its surface, the thirty-two points representing the centers of the twenty triangular faces of an icosahedron interwoven with the twelve pentagonal faces of a dodecahedron. The high-explosive shells of nuclear weapons have the same surface configuration— alternating pentagons and hexagons—as soccer balls. Alvarez used a high-voltage capacitor discharge to explode fine wires imbedded in the explosive blocks.

4. I. I. Rabi, *Science: the Center of Culture* (World, 1970), 138.

surrender before that deadline then Japan would not have to be divided as Germany had been divided into Soviet and Western spheres of influence—and the Soviets, U.S. leaders imagined, might be deterred from postwar adventures.

The Japanese had begun inquiring of the Soviets about the possibility of negotiating surrender, but official Allied policy demanded that surrender be unconditional. "We faced a terrible decision," Truman's Secretary of State, James Byrnes, wrote after the war. "We could not rely on Japan's inquiries to the Soviet Union about a negotiated peace as proof that Japan would surrender unconditionally without the use of the bomb. In fact, Stalin stated the last message to him had said that Japan would 'fight to the death rather than accept unconditional surrender.' Under the circumstances, agreement to negotiate could only arouse false hopes."[5]

The atomic bombs had cost more than two billion dollars in black-budget funds to build, an expense that the head of the Manhattan Project, Brigadier General Leslie R. Groves, among others, believed only use could justify to the U. S. Congress.

Some favored use to demonstrate to the world what terrors the future would hold. "Our only hope," Edward Teller wrote Leo Szilard to explain why he chose not to sign a petition of protest Szilard had sent him, "is in getting the facts of our results before the people. This might help to convince everybody that the next war would be fatal. For this purpose actual combat-use might even be the best thing."[6]

The secretary of war, Henry Stimson, assigned a scientific panel the unenviable task of inventing a demonstration sufficiently credible to convince the Japanese to surrender. The panel—Nobel laureate physicists Ernest Lawrence, Arthur Compton, and Enrico Fermi, along with Los Alamos director Robert Oppenheimer, knowledgeable, intelligent, morally responsible men—agonized across a June weekend and concluded, "we can propose no technical demonstration likely to bring an end to the war; we see no acceptable alternative to direct military use."[7]

The decision was finally military. Against the background of the systematic firebombing of Japan, a horror of mass destruction that had been ongoing since the previous April, it did not seem a qualitative

5. James Byrnes, *Speaking Frankly* (Harper & Bros., 1947), 262.

6. ET to LS, July 2, 1945. Manhattan Engineer District Records (Record Group 77), National Archives, Washington, D.C., MED 201, Leo Szilard.

7. Manhattan Engineer District Records, op. cit., MED 76.

escalation. Fleets of B-29s flying low over Japanese cities were drop-
ping thousands of six-pound incendiary bombs on Japan's flimsy wood
and rice-paper housing that started deadly firestorms; by the end of the
war, the firebombing campaign had burned out sixty-eight cities and
caused hundreds of thousands of civilian deaths.[8] Hiroshima and Nagasaki only survived intact for atomic bombing because the Army Air
Force had been ordered to set them aside.

The atomic bombs exploded over Hiroshima on August 6, 1945,
and Nagasaki on August 9, 1945, decisively ended the war. The Japanese emperor, in a formal broadcast to his people on August 15
asking them to lay down their arms, specifically cited "a new and most
cruel bomb" as "the reason why We have [surrendered]."[9]

The destruction of two populous cities with only two bombs revealed to the world, shockingly, that science had drilled a well into an
essentially inexhaustible source of energy.[10] Niels Bohr defined the
significance of that change once in a single sentence: "We are in a
completely new situation, that cannot be resolved by war."[11] Across
the next four decades, struggling to accommodate itself to the new
reality, international politics moved on a dangerous double track.
American overconfidence when it was the sole possessor of atomic
weapons collapsed when the Soviet Union tested its first atomic bomb
in August 1949. Both nations began stockpiling atomic bombs and
then hydrogen bombs (once they learned how to make them in 1951
and 1953) as if they were weapons that might actually be used. At the
same time, and increasingly as the terrible stockpiles enlarged, leaders
of both nations came to understand that there was no defense against
weapons so cheap and portable and appallingly destructive.

Grudgingly, one after another, without public admission of their
vulnerability, American and Soviet leaders bowed to the inevitable and
found ways to restrain direct conflict between their two countries. "In
the real world of real political leaders," special assistant for national
security McGeorge Bundy noted as far back as 1969, "a decision that
would bring even one hydrogen bomb on one city of one's own coun-

8. The U.S. Army Air Force dropped 150 kilotons of conventional bombs on Japan
during the Second World War.
9. Quoted in Herbert Feis, *The Atomic Bomb and the End of World War II* (Princeton University Press, 1966), 248.
10. For a full history of the development of the first atomic bombs see my *The
Making of the Atomic Bomb* (Simon and Schuster, 1987).
11. Quoted in J. Rud Nielson, "Memories of Niels Bohr," *Physics Today* (June
1963), 30.

try would be recognized in advance as a catastrophic blunder."[12] Rather than risk nuclear war, the superpowers limited the scale of war or fought by proxy in Korea, in Indochina, at the Taiwan Straits, at Suez in 1956, at the Bay of Pigs, during the Cuban missile crisis, in Vietnam, in the Middle East War of 1973, in Grenada, Nicaragua, Afghanistan, and the Persian Gulf. The documented evidence[13] that the United States or the Soviet Union used more-or-less explicit threats of nuclear escalation to keep many of these conflicts contained only emphasizes the point. Publicly the rhetoric was belligerent and shrill, but militarily the response was measured. Actions spoke louder than words, a deliverance for which we may all be grateful.

Because of the probability that a nuclear war would be suicidal, that is, sovereign nations since 1945 have grudgingly but voluntarily limited their claims of sovereignty. War is the ultimate assertion of sovereignty; the nuclear nations of the world have given up fighting at least all-out wars despite the fact that limiting their wars has limited their victories and even led, as in Vietnam, to defeat. Science, going about its business of examining how the world works, discovered a way to spoil war by making it too destructive. World war thus revealed itself to be historical, not universal, a manifestation of destructive technologies of limited scale.

The discovery of how to release nuclear energy and the application of that discovery to weapons of war bought a period of stalemate, a time of truce. The cost in human anxiety and squandered resources was terrible, to be sure, but who can say if the cost was more terrible than the alternative? During that period of stalemate, that long peace,[14] despite the erection of walls and the jamming of radio and television signals, increasingly open communication—another gift of science—made it possible for people everywhere in the world to compare their political and economic conditions with those of other people living under other forms of government. Dissatisfied citizens pushed for change, the burden of the arms race threatened to bankrupt even the superpowers, and finally, with the emergence to leadership of Mikhail Gorbachev and the revolution of 1989, change came.

12. "To Cap the Volcano," *Foreign Affairs* (Oct. 1969), 10.
13. Cf. Richard K. Betts, *Nuclear Blackmail and Nuclear Balance* (Washington: the Brookings Institution, 1987).
14. Cf. John Lewis Gaddis, *The Long Peace* (Oxford University Press, 1987).

In discovering and applying nuclear fission and nuclear fusion, science demonstrated that it has become the most influential institutional force for change—including, pointedly, *political* change—now operating in the world. The *Los Alamos Primer* is an historic marker of that transformation.

The *Primer* remained a Top Secret Limited document long after the war. It became legendary among students of the many scientists who had worked at Los Alamos and returned to teach at the nation's colleges and universities. In 1965 it was declassified in its entirety—properly so, since the information it contains had by then become publicly available in other sources, particularly the widely distributed *The Effects of Nuclear Weapons*,[15] prepared by the Los Alamos Scientific Laboratory, first published in September 1950 by the U. S. Atomic Energy Commission and the Department of Defense and expanded in successive editions thereafter.[16] After 1965 the *Primer* came into general use in college courses in arms control, copied from its original mimeographed form (when I was researching *The Making of the Atomic Bomb* I acquired a faded copy from Kosta Tsipis at MIT), but it has never been annotated and published before. The University of California Press performs a public service in doing so, particularly in an edition annotated by Robert Serber, professor emeritus of physics at Columbia University and the author of the original lectures themselves. The Press thereby makes available to a larger readership of students and other citizens one of the crucial historic documents of our time.

15. Originally *The Effects of Atomic Weapons*.
16. Samuel Glasstone, ed., *The Effects of Nuclear Weapons*, various editions, 1950– (Washington: U.S. Government Printing Office).

Robert Serber:
Preface

Report L.A. 1, the *Los Alamos Primer*, was the first technical document issued by the Los Alamos Laboratory after it opened for business in the spring of 1943. It's a summary of five lectures I gave early in April to draw a starting line for the work we had moved to the mesa to do: to design and build the first atomic bombs.

The theoretical physicist Ed Condon served as secretary during the *Primer* lectures. He took notes, and then the same afternoon or the next morning he'd write them up and bring them over and we'd discuss them back and forth, edit them a little. They're a bare outline because the lectures were a bare outline. Everyone had just arrived. Buildings were still under construction. All the apparatus was in crates. People were unpacking it and putting it together and working twelve to sixteen hours a day. Pulling them away from what they were doing and getting them together for a series of lectures wasn't the easiest thing in the world. The time had to be cut to a minimum. That meant, in planning the lectures, that I had to cut explanations and decide what to leave out, to make a skeleton outline of the information. But within those limitations the *Primer* is essentially a summary of everything we knew in April 1943 about how to make an atomic bomb.

I don't think I've seen written down anywhere how we came to know what we knew at that point. Since I was involved in developing the information, I'll fill in my own background here as well as the background of the *Primer* lectures.

I grew up in Philadelphia and went to Philadelphia public schools, long enough ago that there were still horses in the streets. We'd ride to school by jumping on the back step of a horse-drawn ice wagon. Central High was an unusual institution at that time. The science teachers were connected with the Franklin Institute. They were competent science teachers and the courses they taught were practically on a college level. Strangely enough, I didn't go into the academic program in high school. I went into what was called industrial arts, which included carpentering, blacksmithing, engineering drawing, and subjects like that, but which also included physics and mathematics—possibly more than the academic program offered.

I had an uncle who was chief engineer for the Atlantic Refining Company. He influenced me to choose an engineering college. I went to Lehigh, which was and is a good engineering school. I went as a mechanical engineer to begin with, because that's what my uncle was. But Lehigh had just started a new major called engineering physics, which was to concentrate more on physics than the usual engineering program did. The great advantage of the major was that nobody really quite knew what it was. So you could design it however you wanted to. You could spend all of your time taking physics and mathematics courses, for example.

I graduated from Lehigh in 1930, the beginning of the worst years of the Great Depression. By then I knew I wanted to go on to graduate study in physics, and I was extremely lucky. I got a teaching assistantship at the University of Wisconsin. That was the last year there were any openings for teaching assistants. We earned the princely salary of eight hundred dollars a year. And lived on it. Not so badly, as a matter of fact. You could get dinner for a quarter at the Student Union, a hamburger or an egg sandwich for a nickel.

John Van Vleck was my professor at Wisconsin. The first year I was there he gave a course in quantum mechanics. No one wanted to take a degree that year. Everyone put it off because it was useless—there weren't any jobs. The next year Van had the same bunch of students, so he gave us advanced quantum mechanics. The year after that he gave us advanced quantum mechanics II. Van was extremely good, a good teacher and an outstanding physicist. He gave excellent courses and we had exceptional mathematics courses as well. It really was a very fine scientific education.

I earned my Ph.D. in 1934. A few jobs were turning up by then, but not many. I got a National Research Council Fellowship at that time for postdoctoral work. There were five in the country in my field, theoretical physics. Three of the five of us went to Berkeley to work with Robert Oppenheimer.

I bumped into Oppy—Opje, we called him then, the Dutch version of his nickname—on my way home for the summer. I was married by then. My wife, Charlotte, and I were driving east in an old Nash convertible, a roadster, to see our families in Philadelphia. But they had a summer school in physics in Ann Arbor in those days, at the University of Michigan, and we stopped off for a month to take it in. Oppenheimer was there, and of course, like everyone else, I was immediately fascinated by him. We got a little bit friendly. In my fellowship application I'd proposed to work with Eugene Wigner, then at Princeton, but at Ann Arbor I decided I wanted to work with Oppenheimer instead. Oppy said that would be fine, and he hoped I could arrange it with the National Research Council.

We drove on east, and I started calling around, and the NRC said the change was fine if Wigner agreed. I called Princeton and found that Wigner, whom I'd never met, was in Europe. The NRC said, well, get someone at Princeton to agree. So we drove down to Princeton. It was the middle of the summer and there was absolutely no one around. Someone told us Ed Condon had a summer place in New Hope, which wasn't very far. We drove over and found Condon sitting under an apple tree. He said, "Sure, I guess I'd go and work with Oppenheimer if it were my choice. Do what you want." So we turned around and drove back across the country to Berkeley. We got within thirteen miles of the place before our old Nash broke down.

We worked on all kinds of things. In the beginning we worked chiefly on the consequences of the Dirac equation, the general subject of what is now called quantum electrodynamics. There were lots of other students, of course. It was very lively. We all discussed our problems with one another. I'm not a very competitive person, and I didn't realize how competitive the whole business was. Everybody in Europe, everybody all over the world, was working on the same problems. Oppenheimer and his little group out at Berkeley were competing with the likes of Heisenberg and Dirac and Pauli. It was remarkable, because it really went in parallel. Oppenheimer's bunch did the same things that all these others did, practically simultaneously. Both did great things, but the style was different. When Dirac published—in the *Proceedings of the Royal Society*, say—it was all elegantly written, all the formulas carefully composed, everything just right. Oppenheimer's stuff would come out in a little letter in the *Physical Review*, and some part might be off by a factor of π or something like that. The little things might not be quite right. But as far as the essentials went, Oppenheimer did some of the important things first. Some he didn't; some he did two weeks late. What's remarkable is that the whole group kept in the forefront of what was going on in the larger world of physics.

Then a big interest developed in nuclear physics. Chadwick had discovered the neutron only a couple of years before, Joliot made artificial radioactivity, and Enrico Fermi was making spectacular discoveries about the properties of slow neutrons. We got involved in interpreting the nuclear-physics experiments Ernest Lawrence and his crew were doing on the Berkeley cyclotron and the work Charlie Lauritsen and his gang were doing at Caltech in Pasadena.

Nuclear physics started off with a bang, and it immediately spilled over into astrophysics. We worked on that. I remember Hans Bethe beating us to the carbon cycle that drives thermonuclear burning in the stars. He beat us partly because Oppenheimer was always very close to the experimental physicists. In this particular case, Oppy got some information from the bunch at Caltech about the reaction of nitrogen which happened to be wrong. So the cycle didn't quite work for us. Bethe didn't have that data. He had to guess how the reaction *should* work and he got it right. Sometimes it's better not to know. That's part of the reason why great discoveries in physics are almost always made by very young people. What they *don't* know doesn't get in the way of original ideas.

During that time at Berkeley, in the 1930s, we got to be quite intimate friends of Robert's. The social life was intense. We used to follow Oppy down to Pasadena every spring and spend a quarter term at Caltech, where he also taught. After that we'd go up to his ranch in the Sangre de Cristos, in New Mexico northeast of Santa Fe, for the summer.

We had a fine time. At Caltech we worked with Millikan and Anderson on cosmic rays. At Berkeley we worked on all kinds of things. I worked with Oppenheimer and Snyder on black holes. My name wasn't on the paper, but I was in on the initial phases.

The NRC fellowship only lasted two years. Then Oppy appointed me as a research assistant. I'd been getting twelve hundred dollars a year from the NRC. Oppy managed to get another four hundred out of Lawrence. You could live on that. Rents were cheap in Berkeley. We never paid more than forty dollars a month for an apartment. It was even cheaper living in Pasadena, where a lot of the houses had little garden cottages behind them that you could rent for twenty-five dollars a month. We didn't have more personal possessions than we could fit into a car, so we wouldn't keep an apartment in Berkeley. We'd pack all our stuff, take it down to Pasadena, and come back at the end of the summer and find a new apartment.

When we worked, Oppy would get everybody together in one room and talk to people one at a time and then he'd leave. My job was to tell each one what he'd told them about what they were supposed to do.

Everything was fine, going along smoothly, and then a monkey wrench was thrown into the works. The University of Illinois at Urbana got the money to start a really good physics department. I was offered an assistant professorship, which I promptly turned down because I didn't want to leave Berkeley. Just then I. I. Rabi appeared in Berkeley. Whenever something critical was about to happen in those years, Rabi would turn up. He gave me a talking-to. Cut the umbilical cord, he told me; be independent. He also said it was unusual for a Jewish boy to get a job at a university, which is something that hadn't occurred to me at the time. Much later I discovered that Oppy had been trying for a long time, without success, to get me appointed at Berkeley. There was a letter from the chairman of the department, Raymond Birge, saying that one Jew on the faculty was enough. Anyway, Rabi persuaded me that I really had to take the job.

In the fall of 1938 I moved to Urbana. I was there for four years, until 1942, when I got involved in the Manhattan Project. Urbana and Berkeley had different terms, so when school ended in Illinois we'd go out to Berkeley, and then we'd spend part of the summer at Oppy's ranch. The ranch was almost all concerned with horses, not with physics.

There was a lot of interesting physics going on during that time. Oppy and I used to write each other every week. That's how I heard about fission. I had a letter from Oppy. In that first letter, within a week of Niels Bohr's announcement of the discovery at the Washington Conference on Theoretical Physics on January 26, 1939, Oppy remarked on the possibilities for nuclear power and for a bomb. These possibilities were immediately obvious to any good physicist. As soon as he heard about it, for example, Maurice Goldhaber, who was never allowed to work on any secret project during the war—because he had relatives in Germany, I think—promptly invented a theory of the pile, the nuclear reactor, just as Fermi shortly did. Goldhaber had it all, fairly complete, and he kept trying to interest people in it. By that time there was some secret work going on, and people had to pretend they didn't understand or didn't care. He was extremely frustrated.

So I got a letter from Oppy at the end of January or early in February 1939, and on the same evening at the journal club I reported on fission and the theory of fission. It took a couple of hours to work something out. I went to the library and looked at the theory of the oscillations of a liquid drop, hydrodynamics. It was all pretty obvious, or at least the essential parts were.

The war came to the American universities long before Pearl Harbor brought it to the rest of the country. To work on radar and torpedoes and the like, experimental physicists were leaving right and left, mostly for MIT, where the radar work was centered. As I remember it, I was recruited a week after Pearl Harbor. About the middle of December 1941 I got a phone call from Oppy. He was in the east and was returning to Berkeley. In those days people normally traveled by train, not by plane. He told me he'd stop off in Chicago and come down to Urbana, because there was something he wanted to talk to me about.

I remember the visit clearly. Our house was practically on the edge of town. You'd just walk down another half block and then there was a big cornfield, and beyond that, corn stretching all the way to the horizon. When we first moved to Urbana it was a little difficult getting used to living in a small town. We complained once to Rabi when he came to visit us and we were walking out among the corn fields and he said, "You know, if Cézanne or Van Gogh had painted this you'd think it was beautiful."

So walking through the countryside, Oppy told me that there'd been a project which Gregory Breit had been in charge of, and Breit had been fired and Oppy appointed. It was to develop the weapon side of the project. These secrets weren't very secret. I don't know if I already knew that Fermi was working at Columbia on the other side of it by then, the reactor side. Anyway, Oppy told me that he was going to take over bomb development, and he wanted me to come out to Berkeley to work with him.

I was surprised that a theoretical physicist, rather than an experimentalist, was leading a program in bomb design, but at that point the problem *was* largely theoretical. We talked it over and I agreed to come, but because so many people had already left for war work, the teaching situation was desperate. Who would keep the classes going?

So we agreed that I would come as soon as the spring semester had ended, sometime around the end of April.

At the end of April 1942 we went out to Berkeley. Berkeley was a very confused place. There were big shipyards at Richmond, up the road, and there just wasn't any housing left in the area. Oppy and his wife, Kitty, had bought a house on Eagle Hill, in Kensington, just north of Berkeley. They had a spare room over the garage, and that's where Charlotte and I lived for that year.

Oppy had assembled a small theoretical group. Lawrence had a project going up on the hill to devise a way to separate U^{235} from U^{238} electromagnetically—the project that developed the calutron electromagnetic separators that the Manhattan Project eventually operated at Oak Ridge. This bunch of kids Oppy had put together, half a dozen or so, were working on calculating orbits in the magnetic field and that kind of thing.

We had a few English papers on the bomb problem to start with, which gave a rudimentary sort of general first look at the questions of critical mass, efficiency and so on.[1] They were a great help, because we didn't have to start from scratch. Someone had laid a groundwork, a very crude groundwork, and it was a place to begin. I've heard that Gregory Breit, Oppy's predecessor at bomb-design work, had estimates that were off by orders of magnitude—the bomb much larger than it would need to be, the yield much less. Breit kept everything so secret, though, that nobody ever found out what his estimates were based on. I never saw any of those figures. The ones we saw came from the English. I don't remember what they were, but they weren't wild.

I took over part of the time of the group that was working for Lawrence. They still had to do what Lawrence wanted done—he was paying them—but actually, I'd say two-thirds of their time was being diverted. They came up with a much better diffusion theory.[2] They said, here, we have exact solutions to it. This was Eldred Nelson and Stan Frankel. I don't know if they solved the problem themselves or looked through the literature and found the solutions. It doesn't matter; the point is that they introduced better methods into the project,

1. But not the Frisch-Peierls memorandum that made the MAUD report such a sensation when it arrived in the United States in the summer of 1941. We had some later papers, including work from Peierls. See Appendix 1, "The Frisch-Peierls Memorandum."

2. I.e., diffusion of neutrons through a critical mass. See Section 10 of the *Primer*, p. 25.

and got us a better estimate. I worked on the hydrodynamics, too—the question of how things blow up. I don't know whether the exponential shock wave is still called the Serber shock. That's what people called it then. There was a paper from Dirac on the subject, and somehow he got it wrong. We got it right.

By summer things were pretty well in hand. The uncertainties were in the experimental figures, the cross sections, the number of neutrons per fission and whatnot. But they didn't seem large enough to make a difference between failure and success. They might determine whether the bomb would be a little bigger or a little smaller. I think we were lucky that some of the answers came out within ten percent of the final ones. It *was* just pure luck. There was an even number of mistakes.

Formally, I was working for Arthur Compton—paid by the Metallurgical Laboratory of the University of Chicago. The bomb-design work had branched off from Compton's responsibilities. Fermi was at the Met Lab by then, working toward building his pile. I made various trips up there, mostly with Oppy. We'd stop in and see how the pile was going. It went critical for the first time in December 1942.

The purpose of the 1942 summer conference at Berkeley, which included Bethe, Van Vleck, Edward Teller, Felix Bloch, Richard Tolman, and Emil Konopinski, was to discuss the whole state of the theory, to make an independent assessment of whether the bomb was a reasonable possibility, and to assess how well everything was known. We couldn't have met any earlier than we did and still have had a sensible discussion. I'm sure Bethe and Teller had been thinking about it and probably had seen the same papers I had. They knew the general picture, although they didn't know about some of the improvements that we had made.

The discussion that summer wasn't confined to fission. We reviewed the theory, but everyone seemed to be saying, well, that's all settled, let's talk about something interesting. Edward Teller is a disaster to any organization. Later, at Los Alamos, he would exasperate Charlotte, because he would start a project—a school for the bright young guys the Army supplied us, for example, the Special Engineering Detachment people—and when it was established, he would walk away and someone else would have to do it. Edward wasn't a villain at the time of the summer conference; he was one of our friends, but he started bringing in all kinds of wild ideas. Edward was always full of ideas. One, for example, was the idea of having absorbers built into the nuclear material of the bomb, so as to have one big core with absorbers that the explosion would compress, which would progressively reduce their effectiveness and make the nuclear material more and more critical—what the *Primer* calls autocatalytic schemes.

But the main thing Teller was hooked on, of course, was the idea of pushing through to a thermonuclear weapon, an H-bomb. His idea of a thermonuclear weapon, an idea that he pursued for many years, the so-called classical Super, was one that never worked and never would work. It was essentially similar to TNT—a detonation wave moving through a deuterium and tritium mixture. That doesn't work. But Edward raised this question during the 1942 summer conference and got everybody interested. He'd come in every morning with an agenda, with some bright idea, and then overnight Bethe would prove that it was cockeyed. They implicitly assumed that I had the fission bomb under control, that there was nothing to worry about.

It was a lot of fun, very lively, and of course all kinds of things got taken up. Opacity, for example, which means how light escapes through this hot mixture of deuterium/tritium gas. Edward first thought it was a cinch. Bethe, playing his usual role, knocked it to pieces. Edward had figured the energy that would be released, how hot it would heat the gas, and so forth. Everything looked fine until Bethe pointed out that you would get radiation; you had to be in equilibrium with the black-body radiation, which goes up with the fourth power with temperature, drains the heat right off, and cools everything down. You start feeding something and bingo, everything goes into electromagnetic radiation. Edward hadn't allowed for that. Bethe thought of a mechanism that really drained the energy off fast—we called it the inverse Compton effect—that knocked Edward's calculations into a cocked hat, and they never actually recovered.

Edward brought up the notorious question of igniting the atmosphere. Bethe went off in his usual way, put in the numbers, and showed that it couldn't happen. It was a question that had to be answered, but it never was anything, it was a question only for a few hours. Oppy made the big mistake of mentioning it on the telephone in a conversation with Arthur Compton. Compton didn't have enough sense to shut up about it. It somehow got into a document that went to Washington. So every once in a while after that, someone happened to notice it, and then back down the ladder came the question, and the thing never was laid to rest.

Richard Tolman had the other idea that was really important, though its importance wasn't fully realized at the time. Tolman came to me one day and talked about implosion—blowing the pieces of nuclear material together with high explosives to assemble a critical mass. We discussed it that summer and wrote a memorandum on the subject. We didn't have the idea of compressing solid material, of increasing the density of solid metal by squeezing it. We were thinking of imploding a shell, of assembling a critical mass by changing the geometry from a shell to a solid sphere. That was the primary idea. The memorandum we wrote got lost after the war, but two other memos by Tolman exist, and notes of a March 1943 meeting show Compton and Bush advising Oppy to pursue the method. So the story of Seth Neddermeyer the lone genius coming up with implosion on his own is all hokum. He heard implosion discussed during the *Primer* lectures. The drawing in the *Primer* showing pieces being blown together by a ring of high explosives is a version of implosion (see page 59). Neddermeyer didn't think it up himself. It was Richard Tolman who brought the idea into the project.

General Groves, the Army Corps of Engineers brigadier general who directed the Manhattan Project, turned up in Berkeley in October. That was the first time I met him. I was in the office with Oppy when Groves came in with a colonel in tow, probably Ken Nichols. Groves walked in, unbuttoned his tunic, took it off, handed it to Nichols, and said, "Take this and find a dry cleaner and get it cleaned." Treating a colonel like an errand boy. That was Groves's way.

After the summer conference the members of the group would get together in twos and threes. Oppy and I would go up to Chicago, meet Bethe and Teller, and talk things over again. There was a good deal of conferring going on. Robert began to do more and more traveling. He had all sorts of experimental projects to supervise. I think John Manley took over running those. Oppy had to talk to people and keep up their morale, tell them a little about what was happening. Planning started for Los Alamos, which took up more and more of his time. I was running the theory group, working on theory. There was always a lot still to do.

Finally, things really got organized, and it came to be time to move. That was in March 1943. Oppenheimer left a couple of days before we did and drove down to New Mexico. We drove from Berkeley across Route 66 with everything in the car, just as we'd done going down to Pasadena and to the ranch in the earlier years. Los Alamos was the kind of mess you'd expect it to be at that stage. The housing wasn't ready, so the army had rented a couple of dude ranches down in the valley, and most of the people stayed there. I stayed in what had been the dormitory of the old ranch school that the army had taken over for the lab, the building called the Big House, which has since been torn down. It was a huge log cabin. It had one big bathroom. Charlotte would be taking a shower and a boy would stick his head in by mistake and be extremely embarrassed. The school horses were still around. Bob Wilson collected the job-lot crew of young people he'd brought from Princeton and mounted them on horses. Charlotte and I would go too, galloping across the field, Wilson's kids falling off right and left. Dust flying. The wild and woolly West.

Nothing was organized. Oppy had a tremendous fight with the army to prevent them from cutting down every tree on the whole mesa. He was fairly successful at that. The technical buildings were nearly finished, but the perimeter fences weren't up. There weren't any guards except the Spanish-American guards who'd been on the construction sites. Most of them didn't speak English. There wasn't any security system to speak of yet. The security office consisted of one lieutenant. Los Alamos was officially an operation of the University of California on contract to the government, so Oppy just wrote a letter on University of California stationery to serve as a pass. You'd stick it in your back pocket and go about your business, and by the end of the first afternoon it would be slightly bedraggled. I remember one night when Johnny Williams was driving Rose Bethe up from Santa Fe late at night. They came to the gate house and the guard looked at Johnny's pass, which he couldn't read, and being a real gentleman, he never gave any indication that he saw a woman in the car too.

By the end of March the army was getting some of the housing in order so that people could move in. We moved into a sort of duplex with the Wilsons on the other side. People were arriving. Oppy straightened things out with the army, making sure that they didn't interfere with everything. There was a conference with a big crowd of outsiders. The scene was set for telling people in a little more detail what it was about. And that was where I—and the *Primer*—came in.

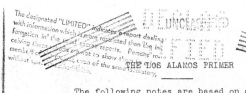

THE LOS ALAMOS PRIMER

The following notes are based on a set of five
lectures given by R. Serber during the first two
weeks of April 1943, as an "indoctrination course"
in connection with the starting of the Los Alamos
Project. The notes were written up by E. U. Condon.

1. Object

The object of the project is to produce a practical
military weapon in the form of a bomb in which the energy is released by a fast neutron chain reaction in one or more of the
materials known to show nuclear fission.

2. Energy of Fission Process

The direct energy release in the fission process is
of the order of 170 MEV per atom. This is considerably more than
10^7 times the heat of reaction per atom in ordinary combustion processes.

This is $170 \cdot 10^6 \cdot 4.8 \cdot 10^{-10}/300 = 2.7 \cdot 10^{-4}$ erg/nucleus.
Since the weight of 1 nucleus of 25 is $3.88 \cdot 10^{-22}$ gram/nucleus the
energy release is
$$7 \cdot 10^{17} \text{ erg/gram}$$
The energy release in TNT is $4 \cdot 10^{10}$ erg/gram or $3.6 \cdot 10^{16}$ erg/ton.
Hence

$$1 \text{ kg of } 25 \approx 20000 \text{ tons of TNT}$$

3. Fast Neutron Chain Reaction

Release of this energy in a large scale way is a
possibility because of the fact that in each fission process, which
requires a neutron to produce it, two neutrons are released. Consider a very great mass of active material, so great that no neutrons
are lost through the surface and assume the material so pure that
no neutrons are lost in other ways than by fission. One neutron
released in the mass would become 2 after the first fission, each
of these would produce 2 after they each had produced fission so
in the nth generation of neutrons there would be 2^n neutrons available.

Since in 1 kg. of 25 there are $5 \cdot 10^{25}$ nuclei it would
require about $n = 80$ generations ($2^{80} \approx 5 \cdot 10^{25}$) to fish the whole
kilogram.

While this is going on the energy release is making
the material very hot, developing great pressure and hence tending to cause an explosion.

In an actual finite setup, some neutrons are lost by
diffusion out through the surface. There will be therefore a certain
size of say a sphere for which the surface losses of neutrons are

The Los Alamos Primer

Note: On the following pages the text of the *Los Alamos Primer* is interspersed with Robert Serber's notes. To distinguish the two, the Primer text is set in bold type; the notes are set in roman type.

The Los Alamos Primer

The following notes are based on a
set of five lectures given by R. Serber
during the first two weeks of April
1943, as an "indoctrination course" in
connection with the starting of the
Los Alamos Project. The notes were
written up by E. U. Condon.

Everybody assembled in the big library reading room on the first floor of the Technical Area, the building where the theoretical physicists had their offices. We had a little blackboard set up in front and a lot of folding chairs spread around the room. Fifty people on hand, something like that. Scientific staff, a few visiting VIPs. There was hammering off in the background, carpenters and electricians working out of sight but all over the place. At one point during the lectures a leg came bursting through the beaverboard ceiling. One of the workmen misstepped and they had to pull him out.

1. Object

The object of the project is to produce a *practical military weapon* in the form of a bomb in which the energy is released by a fast neutron chain reaction in one or more of the materials known to show nuclear fission.

I started lecturing. I started talking about the "bomb." After a couple of minutes Oppie[1] sent John Manley up to tell me not to use that word. Too many workmen around, Manley said. They were worried about security. I should use "gadget" instead. In the *Primer* Condon wrote it down both ways. But around Los Alamos after that we called the bomb we were building the "gadget."

Section 1 emphasizes that our purpose at Los Alamos was to build a *practical military weapon* — one small enough and light enough that an airplane could carry it.[2] There was no use making something that weighed one hundred tons. That was our concern.

We meant to build this weapon by utilizing the energy from nuclear fission. Fission had a history. For a long time before 1939, people were bombarding uranium with neutrons. Uranium was the heaviest element known up to 1939. People had the idea that the uranium they were bombarding was capturing neutrons and transmuting to heavier elements, elements beyond uranium on the periodic table, transuranics. I remember seminars in Berkeley in the 1930s when the chemists discussed the trouble they were having explaining the chemistry of these supposed transuranic elements. The chemistry didn't seem to be working out right. Then Otto Hahn and Fritz Strassmann, in Germany, working with the physicist Lise Meitner, found out that making transuranics wasn't what was usually happening at all. Instead, the uranium nucleus was actually splitting into two big pieces, and doing it with the release of a great deal of energy (and a couple of extra neutrons, as several people soon demonstrated). As soon as that was discovered, everybody realized the possibility both of making weapons and of getting power.

Finally, the reaction we were interested in was a *fast* neutron chain reaction, which I'll discuss later in these notes.

1. J. Robert Oppenheimer.
2. On Edward Teller's blackboard at Los Alamos I once saw a list of weapons — ideas for weapons — with their abilities and properties displayed. For the last one on the list, the largest, the method of delivery was listed as "Backyard." Since that particular design would probably kill everyone on Earth, there was no use carting it elsewhere.

2. Energy of Fission Process

The direct energy release in the fission process is of the order of 170 Mev per atom. This is considerably more than 10^7 times the heat of reaction per atom in ordinary combustion processes.

In Section 2^3 we immediately come to the heart of the matter: that the energy released in the fission of the uranium nucleus is considerably greater than 10^7—that is, ten million times the energy released in a typical chemical combustion such as an explosion or a fire. All else follows from this fact. So we should try to understand where this large number comes from.

We can do so because the origin of the energy released in fission is exactly the same as the origin of the energy released when two atoms or molecules react chemically. It's the electrostatic energy between two

---

3. In Section 2 we begin using so-called scientific notation. Ordinary decimal notation is inconvenient when you're dealing with very large or very small numbers:

$$1{,}000{,}000 \times 10{,}000{,}000 = 10{,}000{,}000{,}000{,}000$$

Ten followed by twelve zeros, ten trillion, isn't an easy number to read. It's simpler and more convenient to tell how many zeros there are after the 1 instead of writing them all down. Thus we write 10^n to mean a 1 with n zeros after it. 10 is 10^1, 100 is 10^2, 1,000 is 10^3, and so on. Convert equation (1) to scientific notation (substituting a dot for the multiplication sign) and it looks like this:

$$10^6 \cdot 10^7 = 10^{13}$$

with the nice advantage that we can do multiplication by simply adding the superscripts, which in fact are powers of ten. We write 2,500,000 like this:

$$2.5 \cdot 10^6$$

This notation can be extended in turn to very small numbers by using a negative superscript, 10^{-n} which means 1 *divided by* 10 to the n. Thus, 10^{-1} is 1/10th, 10^{-2} is 1/100th, and so on. In decimal notation, $10^{-1} = 0.1$, $10^{-2} = 0.01$, $10^{-3} = 0.001$. To get

$$2.5 \cdot 10^n$$

you write 2.5 and move the decimal point n places to the right; to get

$$2.5 \cdot 10^{-n}$$

you write 2.5 and move the decimal point n places to the left.

similarly charged particles. Two similarly charged particles repel each other. There's an electrical force pushing them apart. Work has to be done to overcome that repulsion and push them together from a large distance, up to a point of separation we can call R.

To start with a simpler particle than an atom, let's look at two electrons pushed together. If you released them, they would fly apart with an amount of energy equal to the work that went into pushing them together. That energy E is given by the formula

$$E = \frac{e^2}{R} \tag{1}$$

where e is the electron charge, e^2 is e multiplied by itself, and R is the distance between the particles. The electrostatic energy thus ends up as kinetic energy, the energy of motion. In chemical reactions—the burning of hydrogen and oxygen in a rocket engine, for example—electrons bound in atoms or molecules change their positions, and the change in electrostatic energy is what appears as the energy of the chemical reaction.

Now let's consider the electrostatic energy in the uranium nucleus. The uranium nucleus contains 92 protons, each of which has the same charge as an electron, though of opposite sign—particles of opposite sign attract each other, those of the same sign repel. So the uranium nucleus has a charge 92 times as great as an electron; it's positive rather than negative, + rather than −, but since only the square of the charge is involved, that difference doesn't matter in equation (1). The numerator of (1) is thus 92^2 times bigger than for a chemical reaction. For our purposes, 92^2 is close enough to call 100^2. So the numerator for a uranium atom would be greater by a factor of 100^2, 100 times 100, or 10,000 (10^4).

The uranium nucleus is also much smaller than an atom. In an atom, the distance R is 10^{-8} cm (cm meaning centimeters). The radius of the uranium nucleus is 10^{-12} cm, which is 10^4 times smaller. The electrostatic energy for a uranium nucleus is therefore 10^4 for the numerator and another 10^4 for the denominator, for a total of 10^8 times greater than the electrostatic energy between atoms or molecules. When a uranium nucleus fissions, much of this energy is released as kinetic energy in the two fission fragments that fly apart. Suppose that the uranium nucleus broke in half. Each fragment would have half the charge. The numerator of equation (1) would be a quarter as big—a half times a half. Since the volume is proportional to the cube of the radius, the radius would be smaller by a factor of

$$1/\sqrt[3]{2} = 1/1.26$$

So each fragment would have an electrostatic energy of about a third of the total and the two fragments about two-thirds. That leaves a third left over for the reaction energy.

Thus we see that the energy of fission is about 10^8—one hundred million times—greater than the energy of a chemical reaction, confirming the statement that it's "considerably more than 10^7."

This is $170 \cdot 10^6 \cdot 4.8 \cdot 10^{-10}/300 = 2.7 \cdot 10^{-4}$ erg/nucleus. Since the weight of 1 nucleus of 25 is $3.88 \cdot 10^{-22}$ gram/nucleus the energy release is

$$7 \cdot 10^{17} \text{ erg/gram}$$

The energy release in TNT is $4 \cdot 10^{10}$ erg/gram or $3.6 \cdot 10^{16}$ erg/ton. Hence

$$1 \text{ kg of } 25 \approx 20000 \text{ tons of TNT}$$

To compare the energy released per gram of uranium versus a gram of a chemical explosive such as TNT, we have to remember that an atom of uranium weighs ten times as much as the atoms involved in the chemical reaction. So in a given weight of uranium there will only be a tenth as many atoms. We have to reduce our figure of 10^8 to 10^7 to compare equal weights of uranium and chemical explosive. That means that one kilogram of uranium, if it fissioned completely, would be equivalent to about 10^4 tons of explosives—10,000 tons, 10 kilotons, which is reasonably close to the actual figure at the end of Section 2 of 20,000 tons. (Twenty thousand may not look "reasonably close" to 10,000 if you're not used to thinking in terms of "orders of magnitude," which are factors of 10. Ten thousand and 20,000 are of the same order of magnitude, 10^4; one is $1 \cdot 10^4$ and the other is $2 \cdot 10^4$.)

Somehow the popular notion took hold long ago that Einstein's theory of relativity, in particular his famous equation $E = mc^2$, plays some essential role in the theory of fission. Albert Einstein had a part in alerting the United States government to the possibility of building an atomic bomb, but his theory of relativity is not required in discussing fission. The theory of fission is what physicists call a nonrelativistic theory, meaning that relativistic effects are too small to affect the dynamics of the fission process significantly.

Section 2 of the *Primer* gives a more exact calculation of the ratio of the energy released by the fission of a gram of uranium to the energy released by the explosion of a gram of TNT. To get the ratio of such quantities, you have to measure them in the same units. That complicates things, because in different branches of science it's convenient to use different units to measure the same quantity. A chemist is likely to measure energy in calories, while the standard unit of energy for the physicist is the erg. The erg is rather too small a unit to be convenient for everyday use. Utilities bill customers for kilowatt hours of electric energy; there are $3.6 \cdot 10^{13}$ ergs in a kilowatt hour. On the other hand, the erg is too large a unit to be convenient for an atomic physicist, who uses a smaller and different unit, the electron volt: the energy acquired by an electron falling through a potential difference of one volt. That's a convenient size; the energy that binds an electron in a hydrogen atom, for example, is just 14 ev — 14 electron volts. The energy of typical chemical bonds is just a few ev. The nuclear physicist has borrowed the unit and uses it in larger multiples: *Kev*, meaning 1,000 ev (10^3); *Mev*, meaning 1,000,000 ev (10^6).

The *Primer* gives the energy released in fission as 170 Mev. To compare this number with the energy released by TNT, which is given in ergs per gram, you have to know how many electron volts there are in an erg. The simplest and most reliable way to answer this question is to go to a library and take down a reference book like the *Handbook of Chemistry and Physics*, which has elaborate tables giving the ratios of various units of measurement (thus 12 inches equals 1 foot, an inch equals 2.54 centimeters, an ounce equals 28 grams — these are the sort of ratios I mean). But at Los Alamos at this time, in April 1943, although we had a librarian — my wife Charlotte — and a library, we didn't yet have library books. So apparently I didn't answer the question the easy way. I figured out the ratio on the back of an envelope using the definition of an electron volt and some numbers I remembered. This is the mysterious little calculation that begins the second paragraph of Section 2:

$170 \cdot 10^6$ = energy in ev
times
   $4.8 \cdot 10^{-10}$
which is the charge on the electron
   /300
since a volt is 1/300th of the electrostatic unit of voltage
   = $2.7 \cdot 10^{-4}$ erg/nucleus

which is the equivalent in ergs to the energy in ev. My calculations indicated that the energy of fission of 1 kg of uranium equalled 20,000 tons of exploding TNT—the wiggly equal sign ($\approx$) means "approximately equal to." When I referred to tons I meant short tons, by the way: 2,000 pounds, or 907 kilograms.

In Section 2 I refer to the rarer form of uranium, the form we were interested in, as "25." This simple code was commonly used in the Manhattan Project; 25 meant U^{235}, 28 meant U^{238}, 49 meant one kind of plutonium, Pu^{239}. Uranium is element 92, plutonium element 94, the numbers referring to the number of protons in their nuclei. The sum of both protons and neutrons in the nuclei of atoms gives what is loosely referred to as the atomic weight (it's not really a weight). Every kind of uranium has 92 protons, every kind of plutonium has 94 protons, but different kinds differ in their numbers of neutrons. These different kinds are called "isotopes." The common isotope of uranium has atomic number 92 and atomic weight 238 (indicating 146 neutrons: 238 total nucleons − 92 protons = 146). A much rarer isotope, the one we were interested in, has atomic number 92 but atomic weight 235. The isotope of plutonium we were interested in has atomic number 94 and atomic weight 239. The code we used simply took the last digit of the atomic number and put it together with the last digit of the atomic weight: 92^{238} became 28, 94^{239} became 49, and 92^{235}, as here in Section 2, became 25. Since our work on the atomic bomb was a military secret, we weren't supposed to say the words "uranium" and "plutonium" aloud. That's why we used the code.

Twenty thousand tons is a pretty impressive figure for one kilogram of anything. Seven times 10^{17} ergs per gram is nearly 20,000 kilowatt hours. So one pound of uranium, 454 grams, would release 9 million kilowatt hours, for which my local electric utility, Consolidated Edison, would charge me more than one and a quarter million dollars.

3. Fast Neutron Chain Reaction

Release of this energy in a large scale way is a possibility because of the fact that in each fission process, which requires a neutron to produce it, two neutrons are released. Consider a very great mass of active material, so great that no neutrons

are lost through the surface and assume the material so pure that no neutrons are lost in other ways than by fission. One neutron released in the mass would become 2 after the first fission, each of these would produce 2 after they each had produced fission so in the nth generation of neutrons there would be 2^n neutrons available.

Having established roughly how much energy might be available from fissioning a quantity of uranium, I next began discussing how to get this energy out.

Massive energy release from fission depends on developing a chain reaction—a geometric progression of fission events, one triggering two, two triggering four, four triggering eight, and so on. That phenomenon depends in turn on the propensity of what the *Primer* calls "active materials"—U^{235} and Pu^{239}, for example—to eject more neutrons per fission on the average than they absorb when they're bombarded with neutrons. Enrico Fermi, Frederic Joliot, Leo Szilard, and others found secondary neutrons from fission in experiments they conducted independently, within days of each other early in 1939, in Paris and New York. This first paragraph of Section 3 assumes an ideal arrangement of material where no neutrons are lost through the surface or to impurities. Fission of U^{235} releases 2.2 secondary neutrons on the average; 2 is a reasonable order-of-magnitude rounding of that number.

Since in 1 kg. of 25 there are $5 \cdot 10^{25}$ nuclei it would require about n=80 generations ($2^{80} \approx 5 \cdot 10^{25}$) to fish the whole kilogram.

The second paragraph of Section 3 is notable for a mistake. There are not $5 \cdot 10^{25}$ nuclei in a kilogram of uranium. There are $2.58 \cdot 10^{24}$. Uranium metal has a density of 19 grams per cubic centimeter; $5 \cdot 10^{25}$ is 19 times $2.58 \cdot 10^{24}$ and is thus the number of nuclei in 1,000 cubic centimeters, not 1,000 grams. On the other hand, 2^{80} is not $5 \cdot 10^{25}$ but $1.2 \cdot 10^{24}$. So 80 generations is still the right answer (81 if you want to be cranky about it). Since fission occurs in about 10^{-8} seconds, those 80 generations would pass in .8 microseconds: it would take less than a millionth of a second to fission a kilogram of uranium.

In these notes I use the verb "to fission." In the *Primer* we used the verb "to fish." That's some indication of how new our work was. Otto Frisch and Lise Meitner named the new nuclear reaction they confirmed in 1939 "fission," borrowing the word from biology. We hadn't settled on a verb form of the noun yet. "To fish" didn't stick. Today we say "to fission," but we kept the pronunciation: it's "*fishin'*," not "*fizj-un*."

While this is going on the energy release is making the material very hot, developing great pressure and hence tending to cause an explosion.

The statements in Section 2 tend to be laconic. If the reaction proceeded at 10 percent efficiency, it would heat the uranium initially, in less than a millionth of a second, to a temperature of about 10^{10} degrees Celsius—about 10 billion degrees. The pressure develops accordingly, and the explosion is correspondingly powerful.

In an actual finite setup, some neutrons are lost by diffusion out through the surface. There will be therefore a certain size of say a sphere for which the surface losses of neutrons are just sufficient to stop the chain reaction. This radius depends on the density. As the reaction proceeds the material tends to expand, increasing the required minimum size faster than the actual size increases.
The whole question of whether an effective explosion is made depends on whether the reaction is stopped by this tendency before an appreciable fraction of the active material has fished.

As the sphere expands, the density of the material within it drops, which simply means that the atoms are further apart. The distance a neutron moves between nuclear collisions increases and as a result more neutrons escape through the surface before making another fission. As the expansion proceeds, more and more neutrons escape, until the loss is enough to stop the chain reaction. This process is described in more detail in Section 13.

Note that the energy released per fission is large compared to the total binding energy of the electrons in any atom. In consequence, even if but ½% of the available energy is released the material is very highly ionized and the temperature is raised to the order of $40 \cdot 10^6$ degrees. If 1% is released the mean speed of the nuclear particles is of the order of 10^8 cm/sec. Expansion of a few centimeters will stop the reaction, so the whole reaction must occur in about $5 \cdot 10^{-8}$ sec otherwise the material will have blown out enough to stop it.

Now the speed of a 1 Mev neutron is about $1.4 \cdot 10^9$ cm/sec and the mean free path between fissions is about 13 cm so the mean time between fissions is about 10^{-8} sec. Since only the last few generations will release enough energy to produce much expansion, it is just possible for the reaction to occur to an interesting extent before it is stopped by the spreading of the active material.

It should be realized that at temperatures of tens of millions of degrees the uranium is no longer a metal but has been converted to a gas, a gas at tremendous pressure which will expand very rapidly. We can estimate the velocity of expansion for 1 percent energy release from the relation

$$E = \tfrac{1}{2}Mv^2 \tag{2}$$

where E is energy, M mass and v velocity. Using the figures for the energy released per fission and for the mass of a uranium atom given in Section 2, we do a little calculation:

$$E = 1\% \text{ of fission energy}$$
$$= .01 \cdot 2.7 \times 10^{-4} = 2.7 \cdot 10^{-6} \text{ ergs}$$
$$M = 3.88 \cdot 10^{-22} \text{ gm}$$
$$v^2 = 2E/M = 1.4 \cdot 10^{16}$$
$$v = 1.2 \cdot 10^8 \text{ cm/sec} \tag{3}$$

and we find that the velocity of the nuclear particles would indeed be about 10^8 cm/sec. This estimate assumes that all the energy is transformed into energy of expansion, which is not literally true but is an adequate assumption for an order-of-magnitude estimate. In any event, the velocity of expansion can't be *greater* than the number we've derived. That I based my calculations on the assumption of releasing only 1 percent of the fission energy indicates that in 1943 we would have been satisfied with quite low efficiencies.

In these paragraphs we also run into the technical term "mean free path." Since the concepts of mean free path and cross section are essential to the rest of the discussion, they need to be explained. Both concern the likelihood that a neutron will encounter and fission a uranium atom. (For a more detailed technical discussion, see endnote 1.)

The *mean free path* is a number derived by measurement: the distance a neutron traveling through a mass of material such as uranium moves, on the average, before colliding with a nucleus of that material.

Cross section is the area of the nucleus, πR^2 ($3 \cdot 10^{-24}$ cm^2). This is the area that the neutron has to hit, the *geometrical cross section*. When a neutron strikes a uranium nucleus, it's temporarily absorbed to make a nucleus with one extra neutron. Then one of several things can happen. A certain fraction of the time, the combined nucleus fissions, with a corresponding release of energy and ejection of secondary neutrons. A certain fraction of the time a neutron is emitted with lower energy than the original neutron, a process called inelastic scattering.

The *fission cross section* is the fraction that leads to fission times the geometrical cross section (that is, times πR^2). The *inelastic cross section* is the fraction that leads to inelastic scattering times the geometrical cross section. The sum of these numbers adds up to the geometrical cross section.

But this description is not quite exact. I've been discussing a purely geometrical picture of the nucleus. There is a quantum mechanical effect which causes the path of a neutron that just misses the edge of a nucleus to be bent. The neutron comes out with unchanged energy but in a different direction. This is called elastic scattering and the cross section for its occurrence is called the *elastic cross section*. The *total cross section*, the sum of the fission, inelastic and elastic cross sections, will thus be somewhat bigger than the geometrical cross section.

Slow neutrons cannot play an essential role in an explosion process since they require about a microsecond to be slowed down in hydrogenic materials and the explosion is all over before they are slowed down.

The last paragraph in Section 3, concerning slow neutrons, will be clearer after we look at figure 1 in Section 4 of the *Primer*. Let's skip it for now and return to it then.

4. Fission Cross-sections

The materials in question are U =25, U =28 and element 94^{239} =49 and some others of lesser interest.

Ordinary uranium as it occurs in nature contains about 1/140 of 25, the rest being 28 except for a very small amount of 24.

When I reread the first sentence of Section 4 I was struck by the phrase "element 94^{239} =49" where the structure of the sentence seemed to demand "Pu =49." I checked and discovered that the word "plutonium" is never used in the *Primer*. Glenn Seaborg proposed the name in 1942. I wonder if I was aware of it yet in April 1943.

The second paragraph of Section 4 conceals a very great effort of human enterprise. In order to make an atomic bomb with uranium the United States had to separate the 1/140th part of U^{235} from the 139 parts of U^{238} in natural uranium when the only difference between the two for purposes of separating them was their mass. Most of the two billion dollars that the wartime program to develop the atomic bomb—the Manhattan Project—spent was invested in building the vast machinery necessary to separate uranium. One system, gaseous diffusion, converted natural uranium to a gas and then relied on the two isotopes' differing rates of diffusion across a porous barrier to accomplish the separation, but the difference is so slight it required a cascade of several thousand barrier tanks, the largest of them 1,000 gallons in volume, to enrich the product to bomb grade. The building that held the gaseous-diffusion plant at Oak Ridge, Tennessee, was correspondingly large—a U-shaped structure with each leg of the U nearly half a mile long. Another system, electromagnetic separation, relied on the fact that an electrically charged atom traveling through a magnetic field moves in a circle at a radius determined by its mass. Ions of a vaporous uranium compound projected through a strong magnetic field inside a curved vacuum tank separate into two beams, with lighter U^{235} atoms following a narrower arc than heavier U^{238} atoms. Metal pockets set at the end of the thousands of tanks built at Oak Ridge collected each beam of isotopes separately in the form of metal flakes. The system was notoriously inefficient, but it got the job done. Most of the uranium used in the Hiroshima bomb was separated this way.

Another great effort was required to produce plutonium. This element does not occur naturally but has to be manufactured in a nuclear reactor. In the reactor, fission neutrons are slowed down in graphite (carbon) and some of them are captured in U^{238} to produce the isotope U^{239} (since a neutron is added, the atomic weight increases by one). The U^{239} spontaneously beta-decays, a process in which a neutron in the nucleus changes to a proton and emits an electron. Since there is now one more proton, the atomic number increases by one— 92^{239} becomes 93^{239}. This element, with atomic number 93, is called neptunium. The Np^{239} beta-decays in its turn and becomes 94^{239}, the needed bomb material. To produce the plutonium, the DuPont Company under contract with the army built three nuclear reactors on a

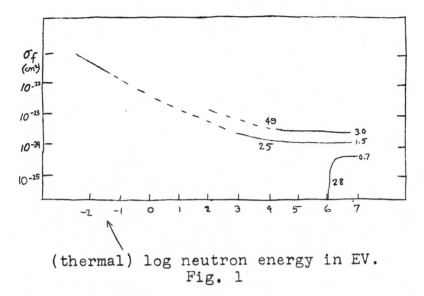

(thermal) log neutron energy in EV.
Fig. 1

780-square-mile site beside the Columbia River (for cooling water) at Hanford, Washington, along with huge chemical separation plants to extract the plutonium from the neutron-irradiated uranium.

The nuclear cross-section for fission of the two kinds of U and of 49 is shown roughly in Fig. 1 where σ_f is plotted against the log of the incident neutron's energy. We see that 25 has a cross-section of about $\sigma_f = 1.5 \cdot 10^{-24}$ cm² for neutron energies exceeding 0.5 MEV and rises to much higher values at low neutron energies ($\sigma_f = 640 \cdot 10^{-24}$ cm² for thermal neutrons). For 28 however a threshold energy of 1 MEV occurs below which $\sigma_f=0$. Above the threshold σ_f is fairly constant and equal to $0.7 \cdot 10^{-24}$ cm².

Now we come to figure 1, which plots the fission cross sections of U^{238}, U^{235}, and Pu^{239} against the neutron energy. The energy scale, the horizontal coordinate, is labeled "log neutron energy in EV." That means the numbers on the horizontal scale give the neutron energy in powers of 10 electron volts. Six, for example, means 10^6 ev, which is to say 1,000,000 ev or 1 Mev. One means 10^1 ev, which is 10 electron volts. Zero means 10^0, 1 ev. Minus two means 10^{-2}, a hundredth of an electron volt.

The vertical scale, σ_f, the fission cross section, is also a logarithmic scale; each unit going up represents an increase in cross section of a factor of 10.

The graph reveals a rather astonishing fact, that for neutrons of low energy—thermal neutrons with an energy of about 1/40th of an electron volt, room-temperature neutrons—the U^{235} cross section for fission is very much larger than its geometrical cross section. Geometrical cross section is the geometrical area of the nucleus; a cross section of $640 \cdot 10^{-24}$ cm^2 for fission is two hundred times that area. It's as if a target on an archery range expanded from three feet in diameter to forty feet in diameter for arrows fired slowly enough.

In the earlier discussion of cross sections we were thinking of neutrons with energies of about 1 Mev, the kind of neutrons involved in the gadget's explosion. For 1 Mev neutrons the geometrical picture of the collision is not an unreasonable estimate. But for thermal neutrons—slow neutrons, neutrons of 1 ev or less—the geometrical picture is completely misleading. Quantum-mechanical effects—the fact that particles have wave-like aspects—become all-important. In this regime, it's possible, and has actually been observed, as figure 1 shows, for the fission cross section to be very much larger than the geometrical cross section. The possibility of such paradoxical behavior stems from the uncertainty principle of quantum mechanics, which says that a particle's position is uncertain within the distance of a wavelength. For a thermal neutron the wavelength is $1.6 \cdot 10^{-9}$ cm; a neutron expected to pass at this large distance from the nucleus still has a chance of interacting with it. The wavelength is inversely proportional to the particle's velocity, so as the velocity increases the wavelength decreases. For a 1 Mev neutron it's only $2.5 \cdot 10^{-13}$ cm.

Which brings us back to the last paragraph of Section 3. Since the fission cross section of U^{235} is so much larger for slow neutrons, can't we take advantage of this fact in our gadget? One might think of adding materials that slow down the neutrons as rapidly as possible. Hydrogen is the best material for slowing down neutrons rapidly. That's the reference in the last paragraph of Section 3 to "hydrogenic materials." Unfortunately, slow neutrons really are slow, and therefore take much too long to do anything. Given the velocity of expansion we calculated in Section 3 (equation 3), the explosion would be all over before slow neutrons even knew what happened. The atomic bomb works with *fast* neutrons. That makes it distinctly different from a commercial nuclear-power reactor, which works with *slow* neutrons. The generations of a chain reaction in a commercial power reactor

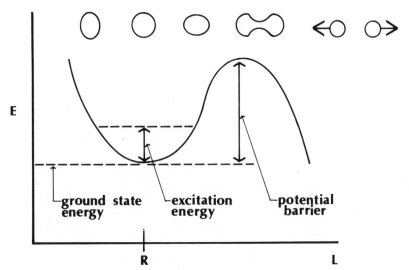

multiply on a scale of seconds. Those of a nuclear weapon multiply on a scale of hundredths of microseconds.

To understand the difference in behavior of the three isotopes charted in figure 1 ("49" is Pu^{239}, "25" is U^{235}, "28" is U^{238}) we need to consider the process by which fission takes place. The dynamics of fission are very much like those of a water-filled balloon. If we wrap our fingers around the circumference of the balloon and squeeze a little, the free ends of the balloon move outward as the squeezed section contracts. If we release the balloon suddenly it will oscillate between a slightly footballish shape and a discus-like—or should we say Frisbee-like—shape, as illustrated by the three left-hand figures in the schematic drawing above. If the circumference is squeezed still more it will form a neck and may finally break.

The horizontal axis of the graph, labeled L for length, gives the distance from the center of the balloon (or the nucleus—it wobbles in the same way) to the free ends. The point marked R is the radius of the spherical balloon. The vertical axis is an energy scale—the curve shows the work your fingers must do to distort the balloon to length L. If the balloon is given the energy represented by the horizontal line in the figure it will oscillate between the lengths represented by the end points of the horizontal line.

The dynamics of nuclear fission differ from those of a balloon in one respect: when the excitation energy is higher than the hill on the right—the barrier height—and the oscillations become so large that the nucleus necks down and breaks in two, the fragments are electrically charged and repel each other. They fall down the right side of the hill, so to speak, speeding up as they go.

When a neutron is absorbed by a nucleus it forms a nucleus of atomic weight one larger. U^{235} becomes U^{236}. But this combined nucleus is not in its lowest energy state, its ground state, which would be the bottom of the valley in our graph, point R. It's in a higher energy state, because absorbing a slow neutron provides about 6 Mev of excitation energy (this number can vary by about 1 Mev from one nucleus to the next). For U^{236}, the excitation energy is a bit more than the barrier height—so U^{235} can fission with slow neutrons. Slow neutrons and U^{238} form U^{239}, which has a barrier height a bit higher than U^{236}. The excitation energy is about 1 Mev less, however, so fission of U^{238} isn't possible with slow neutrons. Fission of U^{238} requires adding 1 Mev more excitation energy. This is the reason why the fission cross section for U^{238}, as shown in figure 1, is very small for neutrons of less than 1 Mev.

Now let's examine the magnitude of the fission cross sections above 1 Mev neutron energy. U^{235} takes about the same time to fission after it absorbs a neutron as it takes to emit a neutron via inelastic scattering. Half the time it does one, half the time it does the other. The cross sections for the two processes are equal; they're each half of the geometrical cross section. For U^{238} the fission time is apparently three times the time for neutron emission from inelastic scattering, so one-fourth of the cross section goes to fission and three-fourths to inelastic scattering. The barrier height in the plutonium combined nucleus is lower than that for the U^{235} combined nucleus, and the time for fission is considerably shorter than the time for inelastic emission, so practically all of the geometrical cross section appears as fission cross section.

The discussion just given is based on the fission cross sections as they were known in 1943. In fact, the fission cross sections for 25 and 49 were not well known. The true values for 1 Mev neutrons, as determined by modern experiments, are $\sigma_f = 1.22 \cdot 10^{-24}$ cm^2, rather than $1.5 \cdot 10^{-24}$ cm^2, for 25 and $\sigma_f = 1.73 \cdot 10^{-24}$ cm^2, rather than $3.0 \cdot 10^{-24}$ cm^2, for 49.

U^{238} does fission for neutrons above 1 Mev, and that fission is put to use in nuclear weapons to increase their yield. But it doesn't sustain a chain reaction. The reason why is discussed in Section 8.

5. Neutron Spectrum

In Fig. 2 is shown the energy distribution of the neutrons released in the fission process. The mean energy is about 2 Mev but an appreciable fraction of the neutrons released have less than 1 Mev of energy and so are unable to produce fission in 28.

One can give a quite satisfactory interpretation of the energy distribution in Fig. 2 by supposing it to result from evaporation of neutrons from the fission product nuclei with a temperature of about ½ Mev. Such a Maxwellian velocity distribution is to be relative to the moving fission product nuclei giving rise to a curve like Fig. 2.

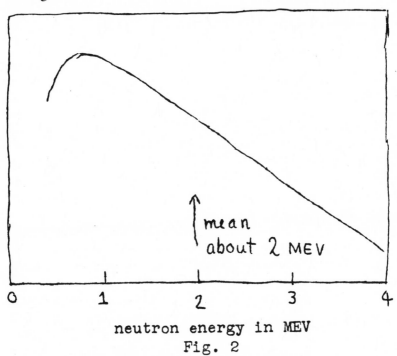

neutron energy in MEV
Fig. 2

6. Neutron Number

The average number of neutrons produced per fission is denoted by ν. It is not known whether ν has the same value

for fission processes in different materials, induced by fast or slow
neutrons or occurring spontaneously.

The best value at present is

$$\nu = 2.2 + 0.2$$

although a value $\nu = 3$ has been reported for spontaneous fission.

As with the fission cross sections, the ν values were not well known
in 1943. In fact, there was no measurement at all of the ν value for 49
and the value 2.2 was used by default. Again, the presently known
values differ appreciably from those used in the *Primer*. For 1 Mev
neutrons the correct values are $\nu = 2.52$ for 25 and $\nu = 2.95$ for 49.
In the diffusion theory used to calculate critical masses and efficiencies,
σ_f and ν occur only in the combination $(\nu-1)\sigma_f$. The values are shown
in the following table.

	σ_f		ν		$(\nu-1)\sigma_f$	
	Primer	*Actual*	*Primer*	*Actual*	*Primer*	*Actual*
25	1.5	1.22	2.2	2.52	1.8	1.85
49	3.0	1.73	2.2	2.95	3.6	3.4

Remarkably enough, though individual figures are way off, particularly for 49, the relevant combination is close to right both for 25 and
49. An even number of mistakes?

This section refers to spontaneous fission, the fissioning of a nucleus all on its own, without the agency of a colliding neutron. In
classical physics—Newtonian physics—the process would be impossible. Unless the nucleus were given an excitation energy equal to the
barrier height, it couldn't possibly fission. In quantum mechanics,
however, there's a phenomenon known as penetration of the potential
barrier. The fission fragments, because of their wavelike uncertainty of
position, can leak through the barrier and appear on the outside. The
rate of leakage is extremely small. Were it not, no uranium would any
longer be left on earth. Interestingly, Oppenheimer gave the first demonstration of this phenomenon when he was a fellow at the California
Institute of Technology in 1929. Robert Millikan was working on
cold emission—the emission of electrons from a metal plate when an
electric field is applied. Oppy explained the dependence of the electron
emission on the strength of the electric field in terms of the quantum-
mechanical phenomenon of leakage through a potential barrier.

7. Neutron Capture

When neutrons are in uranium they are also caused to disappear by another process represented by the equation

$$28 + n \rightarrow 29 + \gamma$$

The resulting element 29 undergoes two successive β transformations into elements 39 and 49. The occurrence of this process in 28 acts to consume neutrons and works against the possibility of a fast neutron chain reaction in material containing 28.

In a neutron-capture reaction, the neutron is captured into the combined nucleus and the excitation energy is carried off by a γ-ray (gamma ray)—that is to say, by a high-energy X-ray. The capture reaction in U^{238} ("28") is important for slow neutrons. For fast neutrons, the cross section for capture is an order of magnitude smaller than that of the other processes we have described—allowing us to ignore it in the previous discussions. However, it must be taken into account in the considerations of Sections 11 and 14 concerning the tamper.

It is this series of reactions, occurring in a slow-neutron fission pile, which is the basis of a project for large-scale production of element 49.

This paragraph refers to the project centered at the Metallurgical Laboratory of the University of Chicago and subsequently at industrial scale at Hanford, Washington, aimed at producing plutonium ("49," 94^{239}).

8. Why Ordinary U Is Safe

Ordinary U, containing only 1/140 of 25, is safe against a fast neutron chain [reaction] because, (a) only ¾ of the neutrons from a fission have energies above the threshold of 28, (b) only ¼ of the neutrons escape being slowed below 1 MEV, the 28 threshold, before they make a fission.

So the effective neutron multiplication number in 28 is

$$\nu \approx \tfrac{3}{4} \times \tfrac{1}{4} \times 2.2 = 0.4$$

Evidently a value greater than 1 is needed for a chain reaction. Hence a contribution of at least 0.6 is needed from the fission-ability of the 25 constituent. One can estimate that the fraction of 25 must be increased at least 10-fold to make an explosive reaction possible.

"Ordinary U" means natural uranium, uranium as it occurs in nature. That material is only 1/140th (about .7%) U^{235}, the fissile, chain-reacting isotope of uranium. The other 139 parts are U^{238}. The point of this section of the *Primer* is to emphasize that natural uranium, ordinary U, can't be used to make a bomb. As we saw in Section 4, U^{238} has a threshold for fission of about 1 Mev. Statement (a) follows from the distribution in energy of the fission neutron shown in figure 2. For statement (b), we saw in Section 4 that when a neutron collides with a U^{238} nucleus it fissions the nucleus one-fourth of the time and results in an inelastic reaction the other three-fourths. Statement (b) offers the additional information that inelastically scattered neutrons have energies too low to produce a fission in U^{238}.

The material received at Los Alamos from the electromagnetic separation plants at Oak Ridge reached an enrichment to 89 percent U^{235}.

9. Material 49

As mentioned above, this material is prepared from the neutron capture reaction in 28. So far only microgram quantities have been produced so bulk physical properties of this element are not known. Also its ν value has not been measured. Its σ_f has been measured and found to be about twice that of 25 over the whole energy range. It is strongly α-radioactive with a half-life of about 20,000 years.

Since there is every reason to expect its ν to be close to that for U and since it is fissionable with slow neutrons, it is expected to be suitable for our problem and another project is going forward with plans to produce it for us in kilogram quantities.

Further study of all its properties has an important place on our program as rapidly as suitable quantities become available.

Neptunium, element 93, was discovered in 1940 by Edwin M. Mc-Millan, a young Berkeley physicist (and, incidently, one of my best friends from the time I first arrived in Berkeley in 1934 to the present day) who created it by bombarding uranium with slow neutrons produced by the Berkeley 60-inch cyclotron. He also observed the 2.3-day half-life beta decay of neptunium to plutonium and an alpha emission he believed to be the decay of plutonium. At this point in his work he was swept away from Berkeley by the demand for physicists to man the newly established Radiation Laboratory at MIT, which was set up to exploit a British breakthrough in radar. Glenn Seaborg, a young Berkeley chemist, and Emilio Segré, who had worked with Fermi in Rome and was now on the Berkeley staff, continued McMillan's studies. In 1941 Seaborg succeeded in the chemical separation and identification of plutonium and Seaborg and Segré showed that the new element fissioned under slow neutron bombardment.

Uranium, element 92, was named after the planet Uranus. McMillan named element 93 neptunium after Neptune, the planet next beyond Uranus. Seaborg followed McMillan's lead by naming element 94 plutonium after Pluto, the planet beyond Neptune.

After the war McMillan and Seaborg received the Nobel Prize in Chemistry for the discovery of neptunium and plutonium. Later Segré received the Nobel Prize for unrelated work in physics (the last time I saw him in Berkeley, he was driving a beat-up old car with a bumper sticker that read, "MY OWNER HAS A NOBEL PRIZE").

It required weeks of running the 60-inch cyclotron to produce microgram samples of plutonium. Even with such small samples it was possible to measure the ratio of the 49 to 25 fission cross sections by comparing the number of fissions in a plutonium sample with that of a sample of uranium foil set in the same neutron flux. This comparison could be done because it's possible to detect individual fissions—the fission fragments make a huge splash in an ionization chamber. To count the neutrons produced by fission is another matter. Neutrons, neutral and nonionizing, can only be detected by indirect means, typically by measuring the radioactivity they produce in passing through material of known capture cross section. This procedure required more neutrons than could be produced from the first tiny samples. That the neutron number of 49 was comparable to that of 25 was not established until the summer of 1943. And it was not until the summer of 1944 that plutonium nitrate in gram quantities began to arrive at Los

Alamos from the Clinton pilot production reactor at Oak Ridge—grist for the chemists and metallurgists as well as the physicists.

Section 9 speaks of the alpha (α) radioactivity of "49"—of 94^{239}, plutonium. Alpha decay is a process common to several high-atomic-number elements. Phenomenologically, it's a kind of extremely asymmetrical spontaneous fission in which the nucleus splits into two fragments, one large and one quite small. The smaller fragment is the alpha particle—the nucleus of a helium atom, which contains two protons and two neutrons and has an atomic number 2 and atomic weight 4. The other fragment has an atomic number two less than the parent nucleus and an atomic weight four less. For Pu^{239} the reaction that occurs is:

$$49 \rightarrow 25 + \alpha$$

If we have a piece of Pu^{239}, it will gradually transform itself into U^{235}. The process is extremely slow. It takes twenty thousand years before half the plutonium is converted to uranium.

The truly astonishing thing about α decay is this long lifetime, 20,000 years. The time that it takes the neutrons and protons in the nucleus to cross the nuclear radius (10^{-12} centimeters) at velocities of about 10^9 centimeters per second is given by

$$t = \frac{R}{v} = \frac{10^{-12}}{10^9} = 10^{-21} \text{ sec}$$

This time provides a natural scale by which to measure the rate of anything happening within the nucleus, and thus we have to explain a factor on the order of 10^{32}, which is the order-of-magnitude difference between 10^{-21} and the half-life:

$$20,000 \text{ years} = 6 \cdot 10^{11} \text{ sec}$$
$$11 + 21 = 32$$

Alpha decay was discovered by Henri Becquerel in 1896 and remained a mystery for many years. An explanation was impossible in terms of Newtonian physics: the alpha particle is confined within the nucleus by a potential barrier. But, as we stated in the discussion of spontaneous fission in Section 6, quantum mechanics allows leakage through a potential barrier, and if the barrier is high enough and thick enough, the rate of leakage is extremely small. In 1928, George Gamov and, independently, Ed Condon and R. W. Gurney—the same Ed Condon who was the secretary writing up the lecture notes that make up the *Primer*—showed that the lifetime of α-radioactive nuclei could indeed be explained on this basis.

Though 20,000 years may sound like a long time, Pu^{239} is strongly radioactive, as Section 9 says. We can calculate how radioactive by dividing the number of nuclei per gram by the mean life (1.44 times the half-life) in seconds:

$$n = 2.5 \times 10^{21} \text{ nuclei/gram}$$

$$\frac{2.5 \times 10^{21}}{8.5 \times 10^{21}} \approx 3 \ 10^9 \ \alpha\text{'s/second}$$

A gram of Pu^{239} emits more than 10^9th alpha particles per second.

U^{235} is also α-radioactive with a half-life of 4.5×10^9 years, comparable to the age of the earth, which accounts for why some is still around.

10. Simplest Estimate of Minimum Size of Bomb

Let us consider a homogeneous material in which the neutron number is v and the mean-time between fissions is τ. In Sec. 3 we estimated $\tau = 10^{-8}$ sec. for uranium. Then if N is the number of neutrons in unit volume we have

$$\dot{N} + \text{div} j = \frac{v - 1}{\tau} N$$

The term on the right is the net rate of generation of neutrons in unit volume. The first term on the left is the rate of increase of neutron density. In the second term on the left j is the net diffusion current stream of the neutrons (net number of neutrons crossing 1 cm^2 in 1 sec across a plane oriented in such a way that this net number is maximum).

In ordinary diffusion theory (which is valid only when all dimensions of boundaries are large compared to the mean free path of the diffusing particles—a condition *not* fulfilled in our case) the diffusion current is proportional to the gradient of N,

$$j = - D \text{ grad N}$$

where D is the diffusion coefficient (cm^2/sec).

Hence we have

$$\dot{N} = D\Delta N + \frac{(\nu - 1)}{\tau} N$$

Assume a solution whose time dependence is of the form[4]

$$N = N_1(x,y,z)e^{\nu' t/\tau}$$

where ν' is called the "effective neutron number." The equation to be satisfied by N_1 is

$$\Delta N_1 + \frac{-\nu' + \nu - 1}{D\tau} N_1 = 0$$

together with a boundary condition. In the simple case in which we are dealing with a sphere of radius R, we may suppose that N_1 is spherically symmetric.

At $r = R$ we would have, on simple theory $N_1 = 0$. (In point of fact $N_1 > 0$ due to the effect of the mean free path's not being small compared with R, but this will not be considered here.) For spherical symmetry the equation for N_1 has the solution

$$N_1(r) = \frac{\sin \pi r/R}{r}$$

provided that ν' has the value

$$\nu' = (\nu - 1) - \pi^2 D\tau/R^2$$

This shows that in an infinitely large sphere the neutron density would build up with the time constant $(\nu - 1)/\tau$. Smaller spheres build up less rapidly. Any sphere so small that $\nu' < 0$ is one for which the neutrons leak out the surface so rapidly that an initial density will die out rather than build up. Hence the critical radius is given by

$$R_c^2 = \frac{\pi^2 D\tau}{\nu - 1}$$

Now D is given by $D = l\nu/3$ where l is the transport mean free path, $l = 1/n\sigma_t$, n is the number of nuclei per cc and

$$\sigma_t = [\sigma_f + \iint \sigma_s(1 - \cos \theta)d\omega]$$

4. Here and in ensuing equations e is Napier's constant, the base of natural logarithms. To three decimal places, $e = 2.718$.

which brings out the reason for measurements of the angular scattering of neutrons in U. In metalllic U we have

$$\sigma_t = 4 \cdot 10^{-24} \text{ cm}^2$$

which, for a density of 19 gm/cm^3, gives $1 = 5$ cm. Also

$$\tau = \frac{1}{n\sigma_f v} = \frac{1\sigma_t}{v\sigma_f} \quad \text{so} \quad \pi^2 D\tau = \frac{\pi^2}{3} 1^2 \frac{\sigma_t}{\sigma_f} = 220$$

Therefore

$$R_c^2 = \frac{220}{1.3} = 183 \text{ and } R_c = 13.5 \text{ cm}$$

The critical volume is therefore $10.5 \cdot 10^3$ cm^3 giving a critical mass of 200 kilograms.

Exercise:
   Show that if the gadget has the shape of a cube, $0 < x < a$, $0 < Y < a$, $c < z < a$, that the critical value of a is given by

$$a = \sqrt{3} \, R_c$$

Hence the critical mass for a cubical shape is $3^{5/2}/4\pi = 1.24$ times as great as for a sphere.

   The value of the critical mass is, however, considerably overestimated by the elementary diffusion theory. The more exact diffusion theory allowing for the long free path drops R_c by a factor about ⅔ giving

$$R_c \approx 9 \text{ cm} \qquad M_c \approx 60 \text{ kg of 25.}$$

   The elementary treatment just given indicates the dependence of M_c on the principal constants

$$M_c \sim \frac{1}{\rho^2} \frac{1}{[\sigma_f \sigma_t (\nu - 1)]^{3/2}}$$

where ρ is the density. For $R \neq Rc$ we have the time dependence of neutron multiplication given by

$$e^{(\nu - 1)t[1 - (R_c/R)^2]/\tau}$$

Hence for a sphere of twice the critical mass the time constant, for multiplication of neutron density by e is 2.4×10^{-8} sec.

   In Section 10 the *Primer* calculates the rate of multiplication or decay of the chain-reaction in a sphere of active material of radius R, and the critical radius, R_c, at which the neutron density neither increases or decreases. At the critical radius the net number of neutrons produced by fission just equals the number escaping across the surface of the sphere per fission. Any larger sphere will explode. The *Primer* solves this problem using what it calls "ordinary," "elementary," or "simple" diffusion theory. The reader interested in the reasoning leading to this theory will find an account of it in endnote 2.

Section 10 first gives, as the critical radius derived from simple diffusion theory, 13.5 cm, and then states, without further explanation, that more exact theory gives a value of about 9 cm. In fact, nearly all of the difference is the result of the incorrect assumption (noted as such in Section 10) that the neutron density is zero at the boundary of the sphere. If we use a better boundary condition, such as the one given by Equation (26) in endnote 2, we would get very nearly the right answer.

When I reread this section after all these years, I was surprised that I hadn't treated the boundary condition better than I did. Thinking back on the circumstances at Los Alamos at the time of the lectures, I recall that the experimentalists were under great pressure to get themselves set up and operating. As I said earlier, it was a great sacrifice for them to take off the time to attend the indoctrination lectures. In preparing the lectures I was therefore constrained to be as brief as possible. There's a big difference, however, between 13.5 centimeters and 9 centimeters—a lot to be taken on faith. It wouldn't have taken very long to have explained a better boundary condition. In retrospect I think I should have.

Quite aside from the question of the boundary condition, the accuracy of the simple diffusion theory was guaranteed only if the net number of neutrons produced per collision was small compared to one. In fact, for uranium this number is

$$(\nu-1) \cdot \sigma_f/\sigma_t = 1.2 \cdot 1.5/4 = .45$$

which is not very small compared to one. To obtain results in which one could place confidence, a more exact theory is needed. As Section 10 indicates, we knew better methods in April 1943. See endnote 2 for a more detailed discussion.

11. Effect of Tamper

If we surround the core of active material by a shell
of inactive material the shell will reflect some neutrons which
would otherwise escape. Therefore a smaller quantity of active material will be enough to give rise to an explosion. The surrounding
case is called a tamper.

We proposed to surround the nuclear core of the bomb we were
preparing to design with a case of heavy metal, which we called a
"tamper" by analogy with the material—usually clay—tamped around
commercial explosives to confine their blast. In the case of a nuclear
tamper, however, we were concerned both with confining the explosion and with reflecting neutrons back into the core and thereby de-
creasing the critical mass. We understood that nuclear material,
whether uranium or plutonium, would be difficult and time-
consuming to accumulate, and we wanted to use it as efficiently as
possible.

The tamper material serves not only to retard the escape of
neutrons but also by its inertia to retard the expansion of the
active material. (The retardation provided by the tensile strength
of the case is negligible). For the latter purpose it is desirable to
use the densest available materials (Au, W, Re, U). Present evidence indicates that for neutron reflecting properties also, one cannot do better than use these heavy elements. Needless to say, a
great deal of work will have to be done on the properties of tamper
materials.

Tensile strength refers to the forces that hold a piece of solid material together and in shape. The forces involved in a nuclear explosion
are so much larger than the tensile strength that the case—about a ton
of heavy metal, as the *Primer* says here—acts simply as a heavy gas. For
the edge of the nuclear core to expand into this gas, it must accelerate
the material in the gas to the same velocity with which it is itself
moving outward. Thus, the inertia of the heavy gas was the essential
quantity we were concerned with. Possible tamper materials listed in
parentheses by their chemical symbols are gold (Au), tungsten (W),
rhenium (Re) and uranium (U).

The active materials seemed so precious that everything else in con-
trast seemed cheap. The notion of vaporizing a few hundred pounds

of gold in the explosion did not strike us as odd. I remember someone at Los Alamos saying that he could order a bucket of diamonds and it would go through Purchasing without a question, whereas if he ordered a typewriter he would need (because of wartime rationing rules) to get a priority number and submit a certificate of need.

One day two smallish packages were delivered to Charlotte in the library. One contained a solid six-inch diameter sphere of gold, the other a platinum disk about ten inches in diameter and one inch thick. These two extraordinary objects went to Charlotte for safekeeping because she was in charge of the document room as well as the library, and the document-room vault was the only really secure repository at Los Alamos, with a bank-style steel door and combination lock that Dick Feynman spent futile hours trying to open.[5] All that day Charlotte amused herself and the women who worked for her by asking innocent would-be readers to "Please move these little packages to the next table for me." The gold sphere weighed eighty pounds and the platinum disk sixty.

We will now analyze the effect of tamper by the same approximate diffusion theory that was used in the preceding section. Let D' be the diffusion coefficient for fast neutrons in the tamper material and suppose the lifetime of a neutron in the tamper is α/τ. Here $\alpha = n'o'_{cap}/n\sigma_f$, with n' the nuclear density of the tamper and σ'_{cap} its capture cross-section. If the tamper material is itself fissionable (U tamper) the absorption coefficient is reduced by a factor $(1 - \nu_t)$ with ν_t the number of neutrons produced per capture.

At the boundary between active material and tamper, the diffusion stream of neutrons must be continuous so

$$D\left(\frac{\partial N}{\partial r}\right)_{active} = D'\left(\frac{\partial N}{\partial r}\right)_{tamper}$$

In the tamper the equation for neutron density is

$$\dot{N} = D' \Delta N - \frac{\alpha}{\tau}N$$

or for the spatial dependence,

$$\Delta N_1 - \frac{\nu' + \alpha}{D'\tau} N_1 = 0$$

5. For more on the late Richard Feynman's adventures, see his book *Surely You're Joking, Mr. Feynman!*

As an easy special case suppose the tamper has the same neutron diffusion coefficient as the active material (i.e. the same mean free path) but has no absorption, so $\alpha = 0$. Then under critical conditions ($\nu' = 0$) we have

$$N_1 = A/r + B$$

in the tamper material and

$$N_1 = \frac{\sin kr}{r}$$

in the active material.

At the outer boundary of the tamper, $r = R'$, we must have $N_1 = 0$, hence

$$N_1 = A \left(\frac{1}{r} - \frac{1}{R'} \right)$$

On each side of the boundary $r = R$ between active material and tamper material, the slopes must be equal so, equating the densities and slopes on both sides of the boundary we find the following equation to determine k,

$$kR \cos kR + \frac{R/R'}{1 - R/R'} \sin kR = 0$$

In the limit of a very large tamper radius $R' \to \infty$ this requires that

$$k = \pi/2R$$

which is just half the value it had in the case of the untampered gadget. Hence the critical mass needed is *one-eighth* as much as for the bare bomb.

Actually on better theory the improvement is not as great as this because the edge effect (correction for long free path) is not as big in this case as in the bare bomb. Hence the improvement of non-absorptive equal diffusion tamper over the critical mass, both handled by more accurate diffusion theory, only turns out to be a factor of *four* instead of *eight*.

Exercise:

Consider a non-absorptive tamper material for which the diffusion coefficient D' is small compared to D. In the limit if $D' = 0$, no neutrons could escape from the active material by diffusion, so the critical radius would vanish and any amount of active core would be explosive.

To get an idea of the improvement obtainable from tamper material of shorter mean free path than the active material show that if $D' = \frac{1}{2}D$ then the critical mass is 1/2.40 times what it is in the case of thick tamper ($R' = \infty$) if $D' = D$. From this we see that it would be very much worthwhile to find tamper materials of low diffusion coefficient. (It turns out that $x = kR$ is a root of $x \cos x = (1 - D'/D) \sin x$ which is 1.17 approximately when $D'/D = 0.5$)

If the tamper material is absorptive then the neutron density in it will fall off like e^{-kr}/r instead of $1/r$ which tends to make the critical mass greater than if the tamper did not absorb.

The distance the neutrons get into the tamper is $1/k = 1'\sqrt{\dfrac{s}{3(1-\nu_t)}}$ where $1'$ is the mean free path and s the number of collisions before capture. Guessing $s \approx 20$ this gives, with $1' = 5$ cm, an effective tamper thickness ≈ 13 cm. For a U tamper $\nu_t \approx 0.6$, and the effective thickness is raised to 17 cm. These figures give an idea of the tamper thickness actually required; the weight of the tamper is about a ton.

The question being addressed in this paragraph is how thin the tamper can be made without significantly increasing the critical mass over that which would be obtained with an infinitely thick tamper. The formula for $1/k$, the distance neutrons penetrate into the tamper, follows directly from the equation satisfied by N_1' given on page 30, with $s = \sigma_t'/\sigma_{cap}'$. The *Primer* describes s as the "the number of collisions before capture," but fails to define it explicitly.

For a normal U tamper the best available calculations give $R_c = 6$ cm and $M_c = 15$ Kg of 25 while with Au tamper $M_c = 22$ kg of 25.

The critical mass for 49 might be because of its larger fission cross section, less than that of 25 by about a factor 3. So for 49

$$M_c = 5 \text{ Kg for U tamper}$$
$$M_c = 7.5 \text{ Kg for Au tamper.}$$

These values of critical masses are still quite uncertain, particularly those for 49. To improve our estimates requires a better

knowledge of the properties of bomb materials and tamper: neutron multiplication number, elastic and inelastic cross sections,
overall experiments on tamper materials. Finally, however, when
materials are available, the critical masses will have to be determined by actual test.

It was not until the early months of 1945 that Los Alamos received
amounts of 25 and 49 comparable to their critical masses. The critical
masses were determined by a series of "integral experiments."[6] Spheres
of active material and U tamper were fabricated. In one series of experiments a neutron source was placed at the center of the core of
active material. The number of neutrons emerging from the assembly
was greater than if the source were there alone and the multiplication
in the number of neutrons could be measured. As more material came
in, larger and larger spheres were made. The larger the sphere the
larger the multiplication. The critical radius was determined by extrapolating to infinite multiplication. In another series of experiments
the cyclotron irradiated the spheres with a burst of fast neutrons and
the rate of decay of the number of neutrons in the assembly was
measured. The critical radius was found by extrapolating to zero decay
rate.

12. Damage

Several kinds of damage will be caused by the bomb.
A very large number of neutrons is released in the explosion.
One can estimate a radius of about 1000 yards around the site of
explosion as the size of the region in which the neutron concentration is great enough to produce severe pathological effects.

The *Primer* doesn't say on what size explosion we based our estimate of the radius for lethal neutron effects. Since its estimate of blast

6. The modern values for weapons-grade materials are:

Critical Mass, Spherical Geometry, in Kilograms		
	U[235]	Pu[239]
Bare	56	11
Thick U Tamper	15	5

Source: John Kerry King, ed., *International Political Effects of the Spread of Nuclear Weapons* (United
States Government Printing Office, 1979) 7.

damage is based on 100,000 kilotons, we may suppose that the estimate for neutron damage was based on the same size explosion. Postwar calculations, based on experimental measurements of the neutron intensity at the Trinity explosion—the first nuclear explosion, on July 16, 1945, in the desert northwest of Alamogordo, New Mexico—gave a radius of 1,100 yards.

In my 1943 lectures and in the *Primer* I overlooked a more serious source of lethal radiation. About 3 percent of the energy of the explosion is released within a minute of the explosion by the fission fragments in the form of gamma rays of about 3 Mev. A lethal radius for these gamma rays for a 100-kiloton explosion would be just about one mile. The Nagasaki explosion was about 22,000 tons and the Hiroshima explosion was about 15,000 tons. The corresponding distances for lethal gamma radiation were 5,000 feet at Nagasaki and 4,000 feet at Hiroshima.

Both these explosions were air blasts. The bombs were set off barometrically at an altitude of about 2,000 feet in order to maximize blast damage by avoiding loss of energy by the cratering of the ground and the shielding of one structure by another. The distance from ground zero—that is, the point directly beneath the explosion—at which one would get lethal radiation sickness was 4,600 feet at Nagasaki and 3,500 feet at Hiroshima. It was estimated that 5 to 15 percent of the casualties at Nagasaki and Hiroshima were due to radiation sickness.

Enough radioactive material is produced that the total activity will be of the order of 10^6 curies even after 10 days. Just what effect this will have in rendering the locality uninhabitable depends greatly on very uncertain factors about the way in which this is dispersed by the explosion. However, the total amount of radioactivity produced, as well as the total number of neutrons, is evidently proportional just to the number of fission processes, or to the total energy release.

When the bombs were dropped on Japan I was on Tinian, in the Marianas, with the Los Alamos group that assembled the bombs. As soon as the peace treaty with Japan was signed at the beginning of September, I was sent to Japan, with the grandiose title "Director of Physical Measurements," to survey the damage at Hiroshima and Nagasaki. I was accompanied by Bill Penney, a British physicist from Los Alamos and an old friend from my graduate school days at Wisconsin, who knew more about physical measurements that I did, and by a medical group, mostly from Los Alamos. We made careful surveys of Nagasaki and Hiroshima with Geiger counters and at that time, a month after the bombs were dropped, found no trace of radioactivity except for a radon needle of the kind hospitals implant in cancer patients. With an air blast, little radioactive debris fell in the vicinity of the explosion.

The mechanical explosion damage is caused by the blast or shock wave. The explosion starts acoustic waves in the air which travel with the acoustic velocity, c, superposed on the velocity u of the mass motion with which material is convected out from the center. Since $c \sim \sqrt{T}$, where T is the absolute temperature, and since both u and c are greater farther back in the wave disturbance, it follows that the back of the wave overtakes the front and thus builds up a sharp front. This is essentially discontinuous in both pressure and density.

It has been shown that in such a wave front the density just behind the front rises abruptly to six times its value just ahead of the front. In back of the front the density falls down essentially to zero.

If E is the total energy released in the explosion, it has been shown that the maximum value of the pressure in the wave front varies as

$$p \sim E/r^3$$

the maximum pressure varying as $1/r^3$ instead of the usual $1/r^2$ because the width of the strongly compressed region increases proportionally to r.

This behavior continues as long as p is greater than about 2 atmospheres. At lower pressures there is a transition to ordinary acoustic behavior, the width of the pulse no longer increasing.

If destructive action may be regarded as measured by the maximum pressure amplitude, it follows that the radius of destructive action produced by an explosion varies as $\sqrt[3]{E}$. Now in a ½ ton bomb, containing ¼ ton of TNT, the destructive radius is of the order of 150 feet. Hence in a bomb equivalent to 100000 tons of TNT (or 5 kg of active material totally converted) one would expect a destructive radius of the order of $\sqrt[3]{400000} \times 150 = 1.1 \times 10^4$ feet or about 2 miles.

This points roughly to the kind of results which may be expected from a device of the kind we hope to make. Since the one

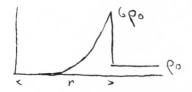

factor that determines the damage is the energy release, our aim is simply to get as much energy from the explosion as we can. And since the materials we use are very precious, we are constrained to do this with as high an efficiency as is possible.

The sketches and descriptive text in this section of the *Primer* concerning the shock wave are correct for shock-wave pressure very much higher than the ambient pressure (i.e., the atmospheric pressure). For shock waves in general, the density, ρ; temperature, T (absolute temperature, degrees Celsius + 273); shock wave velocity, v; and wind velocity behind the shock wave, u, are given by the following equations, in which

$$P = p_s/p_o$$

where p_o is the pressure before arrival of the shock wave (14.7 lbs/sq.in.) and p_s is the pressure at the shock-wave front. The subscript *s* refers to the value of the quantity at or just behind the shock front, the subscript *o* refers to the unshocked air.

$$\frac{\rho_s}{\rho_o} = \frac{6P+1}{P+6}$$

$$v_s = \sqrt{\frac{6P+1}{7}}\,c$$

$$u_s = \frac{5(P-1)}{6P+1}\,v_s$$

$$\frac{T_s}{T_o} = \frac{P(P+6)}{6P+1}$$

Finally, *c* is the sound velocity in unshocked air (1127 feet/sec = 770 miles/hour). Note that the velocity of the shock wave is greater than the velocity of sound in the air ahead of it. You don't hear the shock wave coming.

At a given point, the sequence of events is about like this: the shock wave hits, followed by a very high-velocity outward wind; then the pressure and wind velocity decrease, the wind dying out when the pressure falls back to atmospheric level. The pressure then continues to fall to a minimum. The wind reverses direction and rushes back to fill the partial vacuum created by the outward rush of air. The pressure then gradually rises again back to atmospheric and the wind dies off.

I don't know why the *Primer* terms $1/r^2$ "the usual." It's true that below pressures of 2 atmospheres—that is, overpressures of 1 atmosphere—down to overpressures of about 3 pounds/sq.in. the overpressure dependence on radius is $1/r^2$. Once the overpressure has become small compared to the ambient pressure, we are in the acoustic region, where the overpressure drops off like $1/r$.

It's no doubt partly accidental that our estimate of 1.1×10^4 (11,000) feet for the radius of blast damage of 100-kiloton bomb agrees exactly with the radius of severe blast damage deduced by scaling up measurements at Nagasaki and Hiroshima to the higher energy. For a 20,000-ton bomb, representative of the Japanese explosions, the radius of severe blast damage is 6,000 feet. At these distances, the overpressure in the shock wave is 5.2 pounds per square inch. The duration of the positive pressure pulse is 1 second. Under those conditions, for a rectangular building facing a shock wave coming from the north, the pressure on the east and west walls would be 5 psi. On the north wall, because of the wind behind the shock wave, the pressure would be higher—12 psi. The wind velocity behind the shock wave would be 165 mph. The shock-wave velocity would be 875 mph. Blast and fire damage to a majority of homes extends to 10,000 feet. Light damage, such as breaking windows, occurs to 8 miles. (Bill Penney thought of taking blast-pressure measurements at large distances by seeing how far away from ground zero the paper panels on Japanese doors and windows were broken. He took an interpreter and a jeep and drove out of Nagasaki. When he found a perfect example— half the panels pushed out, half intact, the following exchange with the woman of the house occurred.

Penney: "Atomic bomb?"

Woman: "No. Small boy.")

I missed another important source of damage, one which was identified and studied by the Damage Group of the Theoretical Division at Los Alamos in the ensuing months. This was the so-called ball of fire. The energy released by the bomb heats a sphere of air around the point of explosion to incandescence. For a 20,000-ton explosion, the radius of this ball of fire after 3/10ths of a second would be 425 feet. Its temperature would be 7,000 degrees Celsius. For comparison, the temperature at the surface of the sun is 5,500 degrees C. The fireball remains at this high temperature for about half a second and then fades out about three seconds after the explosion.

The ball of fire radiates enormous amounts of heat in the form of ultraviolet, visible and infrared light—about one-third of the total energy of the explosion. At a mile from the explosion, the brightness of the fireball is about 3.5 times that of the sun at noon on a clear summer day. It covers an area of the sky, however, about 350 times as large as the sun. So at its brightest the fireball delivers energy at a rate 1,200 times that of sunlight. Experiments have shown that combustible materials can be ignited by the rapid delivery of 10 calories/cm². A 20-kiloton explosion would deliver this much radiant heat energy at a radius of 6,000 feet.

Incendiary effects caused by the ball of fire, however, do not add greatly to the damage the bomb causes. Within the radius of severe blast damage, numerous fires are started as a result of the collapse of buildings, by such things as electrical short-circuits, overturned stoves and boilers, and broken gas lines. This area is then thoroughly devastated by fire. At larger distances, fires started by the thermal radiation are very likely to be blown out by the winds that arrive in a few seconds, following the shock wave.

A much more serious effect of the thermal radiation is the production of skin burns on any unprotected area of the human body. Moderate skin burns are produced by the deposit of about 3 calories/cm². The radius for producing such a burn is 10,000 feet for a 20-kiloton explosion. The radius for slight burns (2 calories/cm²) is 12,000 feet. Skin burns were reported at Nagasaki at 14,000 feet and at Hiroshima at 12,000 feet. Twenty to 30 percent of the fatalities at Nagasaki and Hiroshima were due to flash burns.

13. Efficiency

As remarked in Sec. 3, the material tends to blow apart as the reaction proceeds, and this tends to stop the reaction. In general then the reaction will not go to completion in an actual gadget. The fraction of energy released relative to that which would be released if all active material were transformed is called the efficiency.

The secret wartime laboratory established in 1943 to build the first atomic bombs took over the Los Alamos Ranch School, on a mesa northwest of Santa Fe, New Mexico, for its isolated site and core of existing buildings. The new volunteers called the lab "the Hill." Courtesy of Robert Serber.

Robert Serber delivered the five lectures summarized in the Los Alamos Primer soon after the laboratory opened in April 1943 "to draw a starting line for the work we had . . . to do." Courtesy of Robert Serber.

The U.S. Army Corps of Engineers threw up a welter of temporary buildings at Los Alamos to house the urgent work. Courtesy of Los Alamos National Laboratory.

Leading physicists contributed their expertise: Ernest O. Lawrence, Enrico Fermi, I. I. Rabi at Los Alamos. Courtesy of Los Alamos National Laboratory.

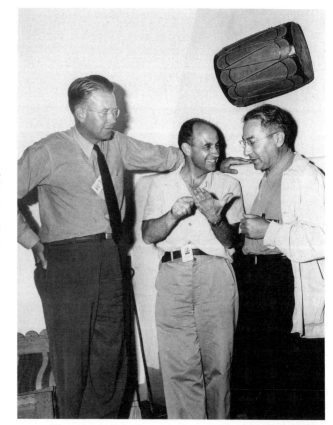

Confined to the Hill, the scientists and their families improvised a lively social life. Here: I. I. Rabi, administrative assistant Dorothy McKibben, laboratory director J. Robert Oppenheimer, and theoretical physicist Victor Weisskopf. Courtesy of Los Alamos National Laboratory.

Electromagnetic isotope separation units like this Beta unit at Oak Ridge, Tennessee, purified weapons-grade uranium for the Little Boy bomb. Courtesy of Martin Marietta.

Experiments at Los Alamos determined the critical masses of U235 and Pu239. Adding cubes of the nuclear elements to a subcritical assembly within blocks of beryllium tamper measurably increased neutron flux. Courtesy of Los Alamos National Laboratory.

Guillotine mechanism for studying supercritical assemblies, the Dragon experiment. Gravity pulled pieces of metal hydride down a wire through rings of the same material. Theoretical physicist Richard Feynman said it was like tickling the tail of a sleeping dragon. Courtesy of Los Alamos National Laboratory.

Sgt. Herbert Lehr delivering plutonium core of first test bomb in its shock-mounted case to the assembly room at McDonald Ranch, on the Trinity test site in the desert northwest of Alamogordo, New Mexico, July 12, 1945. Courtesy of Los Alamos National Laboratory.

Unloading the Trinity bomb high-explosive assembly at the base of the 100-foot shot tower. Courtesy of Los Alamos National Laboratory.

The completely assembled Trinity bomb in its tower shed, with physicist Norris Bradbury, July 15, 1945. Note redundant detonator arrays. Courtesy of Los Alamos National Laboratory.

The dawn of the nuclear age: the first manmade nuclear explosion, early morning, July 16, 1945. The fireball has vaporized the shot tower and is expanding outward, churning up the ground. Courtesy of Los Alamos National Laboratory.

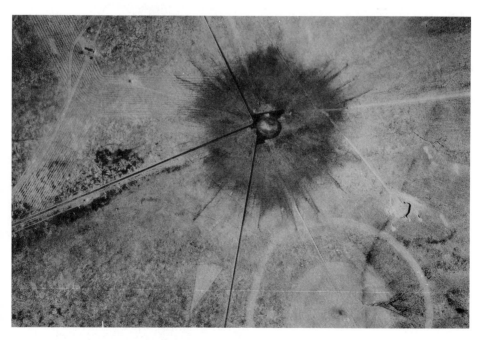

Twenty-four hours later, Trinity, seen from the air, reveals a radioactive crater of green, glassy, fused desert sand. (Smaller crater to the south marks an earlier test of 100 tons of high explosives.) Courtesy of Los Alamos National Laboratory.

Robert Oppenheimer and Manhattan Project commanding general Leslie R. Groves visited the Trinity site and found only the reinforcing rods of the tower footings left unvaporized. Courtesy of Los Alamos National Laboratory.

On Tinian in the Marianas crews prepared the unique new weapons for delivery on Japan. Here, the Fat Man plutonium bomb destined for Nagasaki. Courtesy of National Archives.

The first bomb ready, the untested Little Boy uranium bomb, exploded over Hiroshima on the morning of August 6, 1945. Courtesy of National Archives.

Let R_{co} = critical radius figured for normal density ρ_o, also R_o initial radius and R = radius at a particular instant. Assume homogeneous expansion. Then the density when expanded is

$$\rho = \rho_o \, (R_o/R)^3$$

and the critical radius R_c figured with the actual density ρ is

$$R_c = R_{co} \, (\rho_o/\rho)$$

The reaction will proceed until expansion has gone so far that R_o = R. Therefore the radius R at which expansion stops [the reaction] is given by

$$R/R_o = \sqrt{R_o/R_{co}}$$

Since the ratio of R_c/R_{co} is equal to the cube root of the ratio of M_o, the actual active mass, to M_c the critical mass we see that

$$R/R_o = \sqrt[6]{M_o/M_{co}}$$

and therefore a gadget having twice the critical mass will expand to a radius only $\sqrt[6]{2}$ = 1.12 times its original radius before the reaction stops.

The next problem is to find a simple expression for the time taken for this expansion to occur, since we already know how to calculate the time constant v'/τ of the reaction. Of course v' is not a constant during the expansion since its value depends on the radius but this point will be ignored at first.

At a place where we have N neutrons/cm^3 there will be N/τ fissions/cm^3 sec and therefore if ϵ is the energy release in erg/fission, the volume rate of energy generation is $(\epsilon/\tau)N$. Hence the total energy released in unit volume between time $-\infty$ and time t is

$$W = (\epsilon/v')Ne^{v't/\tau}$$

Most of this energy goes at once into kinetic energy of the fission fragments which are quickly brought to rest in the material by communication of their energy largely to thermal kinetic energy of motion to the other atoms of the active stuff. The course of events is shown in Fig. 3. The units on the scale of abscissas are units of $v't/\tau$. If there was no expansion, and if the rate of reaction toward the end was not slowed down by depletion of active material, then the energy released up to a given time in erg/cm^3 would be given by the values on the upper logarithmic scale. The places on this scale marked 100%, 10%, and 1% respectively show the energy released in unit volume for these three values of the efficiency. A second logarithmic scale shows the growth of the neutron density with time under these assumptions.

It can be calculated that the pressure in atmospheres is very roughly like the values given on the third scale. At a point just below 10^{17} erg/cm^3 evolved the radiation pressure is equal to the gas pressure, after that radiation pressure predominates. Near 10^{10} erg/cm^3 is the place where the solid melts so up to this time nothing very drastic has happened—the important phenomena occur in the next 20 units of $\nu t/\tau$.

Figure 3 (p. 41) contains a label "radiation pressure equals gas pressure" pointing to an energy density of about 10^{17} ergs/cm^3. The radiation referred to is the "black body radiation"—electromagnetic radiation—that fills all volumes not at absolute zero temperature (the universe is filled with black body radiation at 3° absolute). The wavelength (color) at which the radiation intensity is maximum is proportional to the absolute temperature, T. As the temperature increases it moves from the infrared to the visible to the ultraviolet to the X-ray region. It is what you see and feel when you look through an open window at the interior of a furnace such as a kiln.

In a gas the energy density and pressure are proportional to T. However, for the black body radiation they are proportional to T^4. Because of this more rapid rise there comes a point—as indicated in figure 3—where the pressures become equal. Energy is very rapidly transferred between gas and radiation. At a given energy density it is divided so that the temperatures of gas and radiation are equal. If we go much to the right of 10^{17} ergs/cm^3 in figure 3 the energy is mostly in radiation—any energy fed the gas, as by fission, is rapidly converted. In this regime the energy density, call it E, is proportional to T^4, or

$$T \sim E^{1/4}.$$

This is the stumbling block for projects involving thermonuclear reactions—Teller's "Super" and energy production by fusion. These processes require extremely high temperatures, but, as our last equation shows, to double the temperature requires not two but sixteen times the energy density.

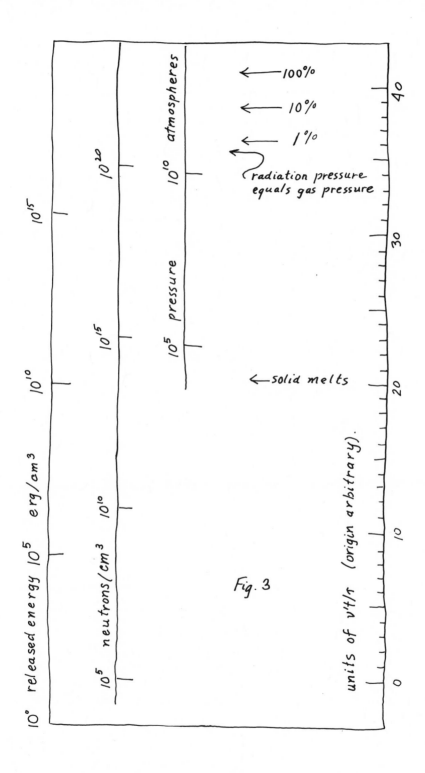

Fig. 3

Very roughly we may estimate, as follows for masses not much larger than the critical mass, the combination of factors on which the efficiency depends: In a time of the order τ/v' the material moves from R_o to R so acquires a velocity

$$v \approx (v'/\tau)(R-R_o)$$

Writing $R_o = R_{co}(1+\Delta)$ we find that

$$R-R_o = \tfrac{1}{2}\Delta R_{co}$$

The kinetic energy per gram that is acquired by the material is

$$v^2/2 \approx \tfrac{1}{4}(v'/\tau)^2 \, \Delta^2 R_{co}^2$$

The total energy released is greater in the order $pV \div pdV$ or $\tfrac{2}{3}\Delta$. Let $\epsilon = 7\cdot10^{17}$ erg/gram be the energy release for complete conversion then the efficiency is of the order

$$f \approx (v'^2/\epsilon\tau^2) \, (\Delta^2/4) \, R_{co}^2 \, (2/3\Delta)$$

or

$$f \approx (1/6)(v'^2/\epsilon\tau^2) \, R_{co}^2 \, \Delta$$

For an untampered gadget

$$v' \approx 2(v-1)\Delta$$

giving

$$\boxed{f = \frac{2}{3}\frac{(v-1)^2 R_{co}^2{}^-}{\epsilon\tau^2}\, \Delta^3}$$

Putting in the known constants

$$\epsilon = 7.10^{17} \qquad \tau = 10^{-8} \qquad R_c = 9$$

we find

$$f = K\Delta^3 \quad \text{with } K = 1.1$$

If this very rough calculation is replaced by a more accurate one the only change is to alter the value of the coefficient K. The calculations are not yet complete, but the true value is probably $K \approx \tfrac{1}{4}$ to $\tfrac{1}{2}$.

Hence for a mass that is twice the critical mass, $R_c = \sqrt[3]{2}\, R_o$ so $\Delta = 0.25$ and the efficiency comes out less than 1%. We see that the efficiency is extremely low even when this much valuable material is used.

Notice that τ varies inversely as the velocity of the neutrons. Hence it is advantageous for the neutrons to be fast. The efficiency depends on the nuclear properties through the factors

$$f \sim \frac{v^2(v-1)}{\epsilon}\,\frac{\sigma_f}{\sigma_t}\,\Delta^3$$

where v is the mean speed of the neutrons and the other symbols are already defined.

In the above treatment we have considered only the effect of the general expansion of the bomb material. There is an additional effect which tends to stop the reaction: as the pressure builds up it begins to blow off material at the outer edge of the bomb. This turns out to be of comparable importance in stopping the reaction to the general expansion of the interior. However the formula for the efficiency can be shown to be unchanged in form; the edge expansion manifests itself simply in a reduction in the constant K. The effect of blowing off the edge has been already taken into account in the more accurate estimate of K given above.

When I came to compose the lecture on efficiency, I seem to have decided that to explain the hydrodynamics of the expansion of the bomb would take too much time. So I settled for an argument intended just to show the factors that determine the efficiency.

Oppenheimer was unhappy with this presentation. After the lecture he complained to me that my description was crude, gave a false impression of our knowledge of the efficiency, and didn't do justice to the work on hydrodynamics that I had done. John Williams, one of the Experimental Group leaders, was present at this exchange, and took my part, claiming that—for the experimental physicist—such a qualitative argument was more convincing than any amount of fancy theory.

14. Effect of Tamper on Efficiency

For a given mass of active material, tamper always increases efficiency. It acts both to reflect neutrons back into the

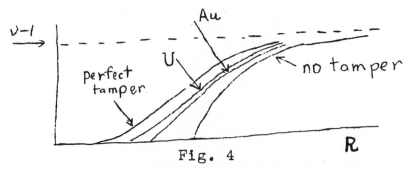

Fig. 4

active material and by its inertia to slow the expansion, thus giving the opportunity for the reaction to proceed further before it is stopped by the expansion.

However, the increase in efficiency given by a good tamper is not as large as one might judge simply from the reduction in the critical mass produced by the tamper. This is due to the fact that the neutrons which are returned by diffusion into and back out of the tamper take a long time to return, particularly since they are slowed down by inelastic impacts in the tamper material.

The time scale, for masses near critical where one has to rely on the slowest neutrons to keep the chain going, now becomes effectively the lifetime of neutrons in the tamper, rather than the lifetime in the bomb. The lifetime of neutrons in a U tamper is $\approx 10^{-7}$ sec, ten times that in the bomb. The efficiency is consequently very small, just above the critical mass, so to some extent the reduction in critical mass is of no use to us.

One can get a picture of the effect of tamper on efficiency from Fig. 4, in which v' is plotted against bomb radius for various tamper materials. The time scale is given by τ/v'; the efficiency, as we have seen in the preceding section, is inversely proportional to the square of the time scale. Thus $f \sim v'^2$.

If we use good tamper (U) the efficiency is very low near the critical mass due to the small slope of the v' vs. R curve near $v' = 0$. When one uses a mass sufficiently greater than the critical to get good efficiency there is not very much difference between U and Au as tamper materials.

It turns out that if one is using $4\ M_c$ and the U tamper, then only about 15% more active material is needed to get the same energy release with a gold tamper, although the critical masses differ by 50%.

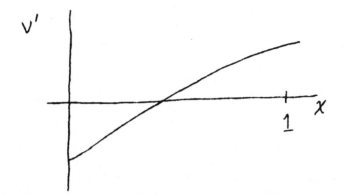

In addition to reflecting neutrons, the tamper also inhibits the tendency of the edge of the bomb to blow off. The edge expands into the tamper material, starting a shock wave which compresses the tamper material sixteenfold. These edge effects as remarked in Sec. 13 always act to reduce the factor K in the formula, $f = K\Delta^3$, but not by as great an amount in the case of tamped bomb as in the case of the untamped bomb.

As this section indicates, the requirements on tamper material and thickness are somewhat relaxed when one considers a gadget of several critical masses (such as the Little Boy bomb) rather than the critical mass itself. The reason is the rapid increase with time of the neutron density in the core. During the time it takes a neutron to penetrate a given distance into the tamper, the neutron density in the core rises considerably. As a result the neutron density in the tamper falls off faster with distance than in the critical mass case. The effect is exactly the same as if, in the static (critical mass) case, the tamper material had a larger capture cross section, as can be seen from the way v' appears in the equation on page 30 for the neutron density in the tamper. As a result the effective capture cross sections in different materials become relatively more nearly equal. And because of the more rapid falloff of neutron density, a thinner tamper is permissible.

15. Detonation

Before firing, the active material must be disposed in such a way that the effective neutron number v' is less than unity.

The act of firing consists in producing a rearrangement such that after the rearrangement v' is greater than unity.

The *Primer* misspeaks here. It should say v' less than zero (not unity) before and greater than zero after.

This problem is complicated by the fact that, as we have seen, we need to deal with a total mass of active material considerably greater than the critical in order to get appreciable efficiency.

For any proposed type of rearrangement we may introduce a coordinate X which changes from 0 to 1 as the rearrangement of parts proceeds from its initial to its final value. Schematically v' will vary with X along some such curve as is indicated in the sketch. Since the rearrangement proceeds at a finite speed, there will be a finite time interval during which v' though positive is much smaller than its final value. As considered in more detail later, there will always be some unavoidable sources of neutrons in the active material. In any scheme of rearrangement some fairly massive amount of material will have to be moved a distance of the order of $R_c \approx 10$ cm. Assuming a speed of 3000 ft/sec can be imparted with some type of gun, this means that the time it takes to put the pieces of the bomb together is $\approx 10^{-4}$ sec. Since the whole explosion is over in a time $\approx 75\tau / v' = \dfrac{10^{-6}}{v'}$ sec, we see that, except for very small v' ($v' < .01$), an explosion started by a premature neutron will be all finished before there is time for the pieces to move an appreciable distance. Thus if neutron multiplication happens to start before the pieces reach their final configuration, an explosion will occur that is of lower efficiency corresponding to the lower value of v' at the instant of explosion.

To avoid predetonation it is therefore necessary to keep the neutron background as low as possible and to effect the rearrangement as rapidly as possible.

16. Probability of Predetonation

Since it will be clearly impossible to reduce the neutron background rigorously to zero, there will always be some chance of predetonation. In this section we try to see how great this chance is in order to see how this affects the firing problem.

The chance of predetonation is dependent on the likelihood of a neutron appearing in the active mass while v' is still small and on the likelihood that such a neutron will really set off a chain reaction. With just a single neutron released when $v' > 0$ it is by no means certain that a chain reaction will start, since any particular neutron may escape from the active material without causing a chain reaction.

The question can be considered in relation to a little gambling problem. In tossing loaded coins, suppose p is the probability of winning and q that of losing. Let P_n be the probability of losing all of an initial stock of n coins. On the first toss either one wins and thus has $(n+1)$ coins or loses and thus has $(n-1)$ coins. Hence the probability P_n is given by

$$P_n = pP_{n+1} + qP_{n-1}$$

the solution of which is

$$P_n = (q/p)^n$$

Identifying this with the neutron multiplication problem, one can show that $q/p = 1-v'$. Hence the probability of not starting a chain reaction with one neutron is $(1-v')$ or v' is the probability that any one neutron will start a chain reaction.

Concerning a little gambling problem, if the odds are against you—that is, if q is bigger than p—then the solution given in the text can't be right, since the probability can't be greater than 1. Note, however, that since $p + q = 1$, $P_n = 1$ is also a solution of the equation for P_n. For $q > p$ this is the proper solution. It shows that if the odds are against you you always lose all of your money. In the case $q = p$, and $q/p = 1$, the two solutions agree in giving $P_n = 1$. Thus Barnum was right. If you give a sucker an even break, you always go broke in the end.

For our problem, the escape of neutrons is equivalent to the active material having an absorption cross section as well as a fission cross section. The game problem assumes that if you win you gain one neutron. This means that we take $v = 2$. p is the probability of a collision causing a fission; q is the probability that a neutron is captured. Suppose v_1 is the net gain in the number of neutrons per collision. Then

$$vp = 1 + v_1$$

or, since $\nu = 2$,

$$p = \tfrac{1}{2}(1 + \nu_1)$$

However, we defined ν' as the net excess per fission. Therefore

$$\nu_1 = p\nu'$$

and

$$p = \tfrac{1}{2}(1 + p\nu')$$

which gives

$$p = \frac{1}{2} \frac{1}{(1 - \tfrac{1}{2}\nu')}$$

We then have

$$q = 1 - p = \frac{1}{2} \frac{(1 - \nu')}{(1 - \tfrac{1}{2}\nu')}$$

and

$$q/p = 1 - \nu'$$

as stated in Section 16.

Suppose now that there is a source of N neutron/sec. Let P(t) be the probability of not getting a predetonation up to the instant t. In the interval dt we have

$$dP = - Ndt\nu'P$$

On the left the first three factors together give the probability of going off in a time dt, and the factor P is the probability of not having had a predetonation up to that time.

Near the value $\nu' = 0$ we may suppose that ν' varies linearly with time, $\nu' = ct$. Hence, integrating the differential equation

$$P = e^{-\tfrac{1}{2}Nct^2} = e^{-\tfrac{1}{2}\bar{N}\nu'}$$

where $\bar{N} = Nt$ is the number of neutrons expected in the interval between $t = 0$, when $\nu' = 0$, and the time when the multiplication number has reached the value ν'. Evidently for a particular type of firing rearrangement $\bar{N}$ will vary inversely as the velocity with which the firing rearrangement is carried out.

For example, consider a bomb whose mass is between two and three critical masses, for which the final value of ν' is 0.3 and suppose that N = 10⁴ neutrons/sec from unavoidable sources. Also suppose that one piece must move d = 10 cm from the $v' = 0.0$ configuration to the final $v' = 0.3$ configuration. Suppose that this piece has a velocity of 10^5 cm/sec then $\bar{N} = 1$ and

$$P = e^{-0.15}$$

so there is approximately a 15% chance of predetonation.

This is the chance of predetonation any time up to that at which the final value of v' is reached. In this example the exponent is small enough that the chance of predetonation $(1 - P)$ is given by the linear approximation

$$(1 - P) = \tfrac{1}{2}\bar{N}v'$$

Since the efficiency varies as v'^3 one will get an explosion of less than ¼ of the maximum if it goes off before v' has reached the value $0.3/\sqrt[3]{4}=0.19$. Hence the probability of an explosion giving less than 25% of the maximum value is

$$(.19/.3)^2 \times.15 = 6\%$$

The example serves to indicate the importance of taking great pains to get the least possible neutron background, and of shooting the firing rearrangement with the maximum possible velocity. It seems one should strive for a neutron background of 10000 neutron/sec or less and firing velocities of 3000 ft/sec or more. Both of these are difficult of attainment.

At first sight there appears to be a contradiction between the statement in this section that the efficiency is proportional to v'^3 and the statement made in discussing figure 4 that it varies with v'^2. As shown in Section 13, the efficiency is proportional to $v'^2\Delta$. (Remember that $\Delta = (R-R_c)/R_c$.) Near R_c, v' is proportional to Δ. In Section 13 this was used to write the efficiency as proportional to Δ^3; it could equally well be written as proportional to v'^3.

At the end of Section 16, the factor $(.19/.3)$ comes in squared because $\bar{N}$, as well as v', is reduced by this factor.

17. Fizzles

The question now arises: what if by bad luck or because the neutron background is very high, the bomb goes off when v' is very close to zero? It is important to know whether the enemy will have an opportunity to inspect the remains and recover the material. We shall see that this is not a worry; in any event the bomb will generate enough energy to completely destroy itself.

It has been remarked in the last section that for very small v' ($v' < .01$), the explosion takes so long that the pieces do have time to move an appreciable distance before the reaction ends. Thus even if a neutron enters and starts a chain just when $v' = 0$ there will be time for v' to rise to a positive value, and give an efficiency small, but greater than zero.

Suppose, then, that a neutron is released when $v' = 0$. The number of neutrons builds up according to the equation

$$\dot{N} = (v'/\tau)N$$

As a first approximation we may suppose v' varies linearly with the distance x the pieces move from the point where $v' = 0$, so

$$v' = v_o(x/d_o)$$

where v_o is the value of v' when the pieces reach their final optimal configuration, and d_o is the distance to reach this configuration. If the velocity of fire is v, we have $x = vt$,

$$\ln N = \int_0^t (v'/\tau)dt = \frac{1}{2}\frac{v_o V}{d_o \tau} t^2$$

Suppose the reaction continues until about 10^{22} neutrons are produced, which would correspond to an energy production equivalent to 100 tons of TNT. Then, at the end of the reaction

$$\ln N = \ln 10^{22} \approx 50.$$

(We can check this assumption after we have completed our estimate of the energy release. However, since the final number of neutrons enters only in the logarithm of a large number, our result is quite insensitive to what we take for N at this point.)

Thus the reaction ends when

$$\frac{1}{2}\frac{v_o V}{d_o \tau} t^2 = 50, \quad x^2 = v^2 t^2 = 100 \frac{d_o v \tau}{v_o},$$

$$v' = v_o \frac{x}{d_o} = 10 \cdot \sqrt{v_o \frac{v\tau}{d_o}}$$

The efficiency is

$$f \sim \tfrac{1}{2}v'^3 = 500v_o^{3/2} \left(\frac{v\tau}{d_o}\right)^{3/2}$$

Using the same figures as in the preceding section ($v_o = .3$, $v = 10^5$, $d_o = 10$) we find

$$f = 8 \times 10^{-5}$$

The mass of 25 in the bomb is about 40 kg. The mass used up is thus $40.8 \times 10^{-5} = .003$ kg, and the energy release is $.003 \times 20000 = 60$ tons of TNT equivalent, ample to destroy the bomb.

18. Detonating Source

To avoid predetonation we must make sure that there is only a small probability of a neutron appearing while the pieces of the bomb are being put together. On the other hand, when the pieces reach their best position we want to be very sure that a neutron starts the reaction before the pieces have a chance to separate or break. It may be possible to make the projectile seat and stay in the desired position. Failing in this, or in any event as extra insurance, another possibility is to provide a strong neutron source which becomes active as soon as the pieces come into position. For example, one might use a Ra + Be source in which the Ra is on one piece and the Be on the other so neutrons are only produced when the pieces are close to the proper relative position.

We can easily estimate the strength of source required. After the source starts working, we want a high probability of detonation before the pieces have time to move more than say 1 cm. This means that N, the neutrons/sec from the source, must be large enough that

$$\frac{1}{2}\frac{Ndv'}{v} \gg 1 \text{ (say = 10)}$$

giving

$$N = 10^7 \text{ neutrons/sec}$$

This is the yield from 1 gr Ra intimately mixed with beryllium. Hence it might be necessary to use several grams of radium since it will probably not be used efficiently in this type of source.

Some other substance such as polonium that is not so γ-active as radium will probably prove more satisfactory.

Evidently a source of this strength that can be activated within about 10^{-5} sec and is mechanically rugged enough to stand the shocks associated with firing presents a difficult problem.

The radioactive decay of a radium nucleus produces an alpha particle, which can cause a nuclear reaction in beryllium in which a neutron is emitted.

After a great deal of effort, initiators were eventually developed for both Little Boy and Fat Man that mixed polonium and beryllium just as the critical masses assembled.

19. Neutron Background

There are three recognized sources of neutrons which provide the background which gives rise to danger of predetonation: (a) cosmic ray neutrons, (b) spontaneous fission, (c) nuclear reactions which produce neutrons.

(a) <u>Cosmic Rays</u>. The number of cosmic ray neutrons is about 1 per cm^2 per minute which is too few to be of any importance.

(b) <u>Spontaneous fission</u>. The spontaneous fission rate is known only for 28 which is responsible for the fission activity of ordinary U. At present we have only upper limits for 25 and 49 since the activity of these has not been detected. The known facts are

28 gives 15 neutrons/kg sec
25 " < 150 "
49 " < 500 "

It is considered probable that the rates for 25 and 49 are much smaller than these upper limits. Even if 25 and 49 were the same as 28, a 40 kg bomb would have a background from this source of 600 neutron/sec. This does not seem difficult to beat.

But if U is used as tamper this will weigh about a ton which gives 15000 neutron/sec. Of course not all of these will get into the active material, but one may expect a background of several thousand per second from this source.

Thus with a U tamper one is faced with the problem of high velocity firing. In the range of moderately high efficiencies, say 4 M_c of active material, it might for this reason not be worth while to use a U tamper, since as we have seen, an inactive tamper will cost only about 15% more active material. Or one might use a compromise in which the tamper was an inner layer of U, backed up by inactive material; for masses this large the time scale is so short that neutrons do not have time to penetrate more than about 5 cm into the tamper anyway.

(c) Nuclear reactions. The only important reactions are the (α, n) reactions of light elements which might be present as impurities. The (γ, n) reactions have a negligible yield. Let us examine what sort of limit on light element impurities in the active material is set by the need of holding down the neutron background from this source.

The problem is particularly bad for 49 since its half-life is only 20000 years. Its mean life is thus 30000 years = 10^{12} sec. Thus 10 kg of 49, containing 2.5×10^{25} nuclei gives 2.5×10^{13} α-particles/sec.

The yield from Ra α's on Be is 1.2×10^{-4} and the shorter range from α's of 49 as compared with those of Ra and its equilibrium products will perhaps cut this figure in half, say $6 \cdot 10^{-5}$. Since the stopping power for α's of these energies is proportional to $\sqrt{A}$ where A is the atomic weight, the stopping power per gram is proportional to $1/\sqrt{A}$.

If the concentration by weight of Be in the active material is c then the yield of neutron/sec is

$$\sqrt{239/9} \cdot c \cdot N_\alpha \cdot y$$

where N_α is the number of α's per second and y is the yield. Hence to get 10000 neutrons/sec one would need to have a concentration given by

$$\sqrt{239/9} \cdot c \cdot 2.5 \cdot 10^{13} \cdot 6 \times 10^{-5} = 10^4$$

that is $c \approx 10^{-6}$ which is, of course, a very low concentration of anything in anything else.

The yield drops rapidly as one goes to elements of higher atomic weight because of the increased Coulomb barrier. So it is unnecessary to consider limits on elements beyond Ca as long as ordinary standards of purity are maintained.

Experiments on the yields with light elements need to be done. One can base some rough guesses on the standard barrier penetration formulas and find the following upper limits on the concentration by weight for several light elements for production of 10^4 neutron/sec

Li	2×10^{-5}
Be	10^{-6}
B	$2 \cdot 10^{-6}$
C	$2 \cdot 10^{-4}*$
N	$-**$
O	$2 \times 10^{-3}***$
F	2×10^{-5}

The effect of several impurities simultaneously present is of course additive.

It is thus recognized that the preparation and handling of the 49 in such a way as to attain and maintain such high standards of purity is an extremely difficult problem. And it seems very probable that the neutron background will be high and therefore high velocity firing will be desirable.

With 25 the situation is much more favorable. The α's come from 24 present in normal U to about 1/10000. If all 24 goes with 25 in the separation from 28 we shall have 1/100 of 24 in the 25. The lifetime of 24 is 100 times that of 49 so the concentration of impurities in 25 may be 10^4 times that in 49 for the same background, which is not at all difficult of attainment.

To summarize: 49 will be extremely difficult to work with from the standpoint of neutron background whereas 25 without U tamper will be not very difficult.

The half-life of a radioactive nucleus is the time that it takes for half the nuclei to decay (that is, to disintegrate or transform themselves through spontaneous nuclear reactions). The mean life is the time to decay to $1/e = .368$ of the original number. The rate of decay of a radioactive nucleus is 1/meanlife. When the *Primer* says here that the yield drops for heavier nuclei because of the increased Coulomb bar-

---

* Low yield because only C^{13} contributes.
** (α−n) reaction not energetically possible.
*** Low yield because only O^{17} contributes.

rier, we mean because the electrostatic repulsion between the positively charged α particle and the higher positively charged nucleus is greater.

In the summer of 1944 Los Alamos received a great shock when the first reactor-made plutonium arrived at Los Alamos. It had a higher neutron background than the cyclotron-made plutonium that had been used in previous experiments. The reason for the difference was the presence in the reactor plutonium of the isotope of plutonium with atomic weight 240, Pu^{240}. This isotope is made in the plutonium-producing reactor by a secondary reaction. In the primary reaction, a neutron interacts with a nucleus of U^{238} to produce plutonium. In the secondary reaction, a neutron interacts with a nucleus of plutonium by a capture reaction to create a nucleus of Pu^{240}.

The presence of Pu^{240} was not unexpected. Fermi and Seaborg had warned that it could cause trouble. What was a surprise was that the Pu^{240} had a much higher spontaneous fission rate than U^{238}. Since the rate of production of Pu^{240} is proportional to the amount of Pu^{239} present, the ratio of 240 to 239 is proportional to the amount of 239 made before the production reactor is stopped and the plutonium extracted. In the plutonium made using cyclotron neutrons, very little Pu^{239} was made, and the ratio of 240 to 239 was very low. In the production reactors, however, where much more Pu^{239} would be made, the ratio of 240 to 239 would be much higher.

It was apparent that the gun assembly would not give a high enough velocity to beat the neutron background. The laboratory was reorganized in August 1944 to apply major effort to developing an alternative method of assembling a mass of plutonium, the implosion method.

The notation (α,n) refers to a nuclear reaction in which an alpha particle (α) is absorbed and a neutron is emitted. Similarly, (γ,n) is a reaction in which a gamma ray (γ) is absorbed and a neutron is emitted. The behavior of α particles in matter is quite different from that of neutrons. The α particle is a charged particle and interacts with the electrons in atoms and rapidly loses energy to them. It therefore stops in a short distance, called the *range* of the α particle. This distance, for the α particles we're interested in, is much shorter than the mean free path for the α particle producing any nuclear reaction. Therefore, the yield per α for any reaction is very small.

It's common practice to express the range of a particle in terms of grams rather than centimeters. The range in grams is the range in centimeters divided by the density of the material through which the alpha particle is passing. It would be the number of grams of material that the α particle passed if the material had been spread out over an area of 1 cm^2. For example, the range of an α particle in liquid air, expressed in the number of grams, would be the same as the range of the α in gaseous air despite the fact that their range in centimeters in the gas is obviously very much longer than the range in the liquid. The stopping power per gram is the energy lost per gram of material traversed. The range is thus inversely proportional to the stopping power per gram and so is the yield of any nuclear reaction caused by the α particle.

20. Shooting

We now consider briefly the problem of the actual mechanics of shooting so that the pieces are brought together with a relative velocity of the order of 10^5 cm/sec or more. This is the part of the job about which we know least at present. One way is

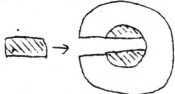

to use a sphere and to shoot into it a cylindrical plug made of some active material and some tamper, as in the sketch. This avoids fancy shapes and gives the most favorable shape, for shooting, to the projected piece whose mass would be of the order of 100 lbs.

The highest muzzle velocity available in U.S. Army guns is one whose bore is 4.7 inches and whose barrel is 21 feet long. This gives a 50 lb. projectile a muzzle velocity of 3150 ft/sec. The gun weighs 5 tons. It appears that the ratio of projectile mass to gun mass is about constant for different guns so a 100 lb. projectile would require a gun weighing about 10 tons.

The weight of the gun varies very roughly as the cube of the muzzle velocity, hence there is a high premium on using lower velocities of fire.

As soon as we gave up on gun assembly for plutonium, for the reason explained in the last section of notes, the remaining gun problem became comparatively simple. As Section 19 points out, 3,000 ft/sec velocities are not required for the 25 bomb as long as one limits the thickness of U in the tamper. One can afford to drop to 1,000 ft/sec, which is easy to attain. According to the scaling law given in the text, this would drop the weight of the gun by a factor of $3^3 = 27$—from 10 tons to $\frac{1}{3}$ ton. The gun actually used in Little Boy, as the 25 bomb was called, weighed 1,000 pounds and was only six feet long, permitting a total length of the assembled bomb ($10\frac{1}{2}'$) small enough to fit into the bomb bay of a B-29 bomber.

Another possibility is to use two guns and to fire two projectiles at each other. For the same relative velocity this arrangement requires about $\frac{1}{8}$ as much total gun weight. Here the worst difficulty lies in timing the two guns. This can be partly overcome by using an elongated tamper mass and putting all the active material in the projectiles so it does not matter exactly where they meet. We have been told that at present it would be possible to synchronize so the spread in places of impact on various shots would be 2 or 3 feet. One serious restriction imposed by these shooting methods is that the mass of active material that can be gotten together is limited by the fact that each piece separately must be non-explosive. Since the separate pieces are not of the best shape, nor surrounded by the best tamper material, one is not limited to two critical masses for the completed bomb, but might perhaps get as high as four critical masses. However in the two gun scheme, if the final mass is to be $\approx 4M_c$, each piece separately would probably be explosive as soon as it entered the tamper, and better synchronization would be required. It seems worthwhile to investigate whether present performance might not be improved by a factor ten.

Severe restrictions on the mass of the bomb can be circumvented by using pieces of shape more difficult to shoot. For example a flat plate of active material tamped on only one side, has a minimum thickness below which it can no longer support a chain reaction, no matter how large its area, because of neutron leakage across the untamped surface. If two such plates were slid together, untamped surfaces in contact, the resulting arrangement could be well over the critical thickness for a plate tamped on both sides, and the mass would depend on the area of the plates.

Calculations show that the critical mass of a well tamped spheroid, whose major axis is five times its minor axis, is only 35% larger than the critical mass of a sphere. If such a spheroid 10 cm thick and 50 cm in diameter were sliced in half, each piece would be subcritical though the total mass, 250 Kg, is 12 times

the critical mass. The efficiency of such an arrangement would be quite good, since the expansion tends to bring the material more and more nearly into a spherical shape.

Thus there are many ordnance questions we would like to have answered. We would like to know how well guns can be synchronized. We shall need information about the possibilities of firing other than cylindrical shapes at lower velocities. Also we shall need to know the mechanical effects of the blast wave preceding the projectile in the gun barrel. Also whether the projectile can be made to seat itself properly and whether a piston of inactive material may be used to drive the active material into place, this being desirable because thus the active material might be kept out of the gun barrel which to some extent acts as a tamper.

In the end, the actual problem for the gun was to assemble three critical masses of 25. We had to be sure that target and projectile were separately subcritical. It was beyond our powers to compute the criticality of odd shapes such as the target shown in the sketch at the beginning of this section. A curious solution was found to this problem. We saw, in the discussion of Section 14, that in a rapidly rising neutron distribution the material in the tamper acts as does a worse material in the static critical mass case, as if it had a larger capture cross section. The converse is also true: for a neutron distribution decaying in time a material acts better, as if it had a smaller capture. If the rate of decay is fast enough, it can act so much better that it behaves like a fissionable material—that is, the neutron distribution within it would be the same as for a fissionable material in the static case. It occurred to me that this could be used to make a slow neutron model of the gun assembly—using slow neutrons to make the time scale long enough so that decay rate measurements were practical. A material with a small capture cross section for slow neutrons could imitate 25, materials with larger capture cross sections could imitate tamper.

Bob Wilson and his cyclotron group built such models of the parts of the gun assembly. They also built a model of a shape that could be well calculated, a one-critical-mass sphere of mock 25. These models were irradiated with bursts of slow neutrons and the rate of decay of the neutron density was measured. If a model decayed faster than the one critical mass sphere the model was subcritical; if slower, super-critical. It was shown that projectile and target separately were sub-critical. Further, by moving the projectile towards the target the point at which the assembly became critical could be found. This was needed to calculate the predetonation probability.

Various other shooting arrangements have been suggested but as yet not carefully analyzed.

For example, it has been suggested that the pieces might be mounted on a ring as in the sketch. If explosive material were distributed around the ring and fired the pieces would be blown inward to form a sphere.

The implosion method of assembly—the assembly of the bomb material by detonating a surrounding explosive—is briefly mentioned here and illustrated by the sketch. As I mentioned earlier, the idea of assembly by implosion was brought up during the summer conference in Berkeley in 1942 by Richard Tolman. He and I wrote a memorandum on the subject at that time. Later Tolman wrote two more memoranda on implosion which evidently reached the highest circles: notes of a March 1943 meeting show Vannevar Bush and James Bryant Conant urging Oppenheimer to pursue the method. He answered, "Serber is looking into it," which wasn't true—at the moment I was trying to finish the efficiency calculations. The notion that implosion was the brainchild of Seth Neddermeyer is television history. But it's true that Neddermeyer was struck by the possibilities and asked to work on the subject, and that he and his group were responsible for the initial implosion experiments at Los Alamos.

The final implosion-weapon design, suggested by Robert Christy, bore little resemblance to our first thoughts. Prompted by John von

Neumann in the fall of 1943, we realized that the pressure produced in the detonation of an explosive could be high enough to compress metals significantly. In Christy's design a slightly subcritical sphere of 49 surrounded by a sphere of U tamper was surrounded by a sphere of explosive. When the explosive was detonated at a number of points on its outer surface a spherical shock wave converged on the metal sphere and compressed it. As stated in Section 10, the critical mass is inversely proportional to the square of the density. If the density of the sphere is increased by a factor of two, the initial one critical mass becomes four critical masses in the compressed state. But to create a spherically converging shock wave in the explosive was an extremely difficult task; it required microsecond timing of the detonations at the surface of the explosive and "lenses" of a different explosive to change the shocks diverging from the detonation points to shocks converging on the metal sphere (the lenses were suggested by James Tuck, a member of the British contingent at Los Alamos).

This was the device tested at Trinity and dropped at Nagasaki. At Los Alamos there was a pool to bet on the explosive yield of the Trinity test. It was won by I. I. Rabi on a bet of 18 kilotons when the result was reported as 18.6 kilotons, an efficiency of about 20 percent. Rabi told me later that he arrived at his figure by visiting the offices of the Theoretical Division and asking the experts what the calculated yield was. The experts, only too well aware of the difficulties of a good implosion, bet much lower numbers. In the event, nearly everyone was surprised.

Fat Man, the Nagasaki weapon, gave an even higher yield, 22 kilotons. Originally at Los Alamos the gun bomb, 28 inches in diameter, was called Thin Man, a name taken from the title of the movie made from Dashiel Hammett's detective story, and the five-foot diameter implosion bomb was then Fat Man. I don't know where Little Boy came from. At 15 kilotons Little Boy's yield was about 2 percent—small, but expected. The order-of-magnitude difference in efficiencies is a measure of the success of the Los Alamos implosion program.

Another more likely possibility is to have the sphere assembled but with a wedge of neutron-absorbing material built into it, which on firing would be blown out by an explosive charge causing ν' to go from less than unity to more than unity. Here the difficulty lies in the fact that no material is known whose absorption coefficient for fast neutrons is much larger than the emission

coefficient of the bomb material. Hence the absorbing plug will need to have a volume comparable to that of the absorber and when removed will leave the active material in an unfavorable configuration, equivalent to a low mean density.

The first sentence in this paragraph should have v' going from less than zero to more than zero. The last sentence should read "volume comparable to that of the active material. . . ."

21. Autocatalytic Methods

The term "autocatalytic method" is being used to describe any arrangement in which the motions of material produced by the reaction will act, at least for a time, to increase v' rather than to decrease it. Evidently if arrangements having this property can be developed they would be very valuable, especially if the tendency toward increasing v' was possessed to any marked degree.

Suppose we had an arrangement in which for example v' would increase of its own accord from a low value like 0.01 up to a value 10 to 50 times greater. The firing problem would be simplified by the low initial value of v', and the efficiency would be maintained by the tendency to develop a high value of v' as the reaction proceeds. It may be that a method of this kind will be absolutely essential for utilization of 49 owing to the difficulties of high neu-

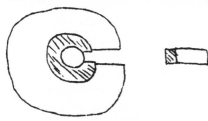

tron background from (α,n) reactions with the impurities as already discussed. The simplest scheme which might be autocatalytic is indicated in the sketch where the active material is disposed in a hollow shell. Suppose that when the firing plug is in place one has just the critical mass for this configuration. If as the reaction proceeds the expansion were to proceed only inward, it is easy to see from diffusion theory that v' would increase. Of course in actual fact it will proceed outward (tending to decrease v') as well as inward and outward expansion would in reality give the dominant effect.

However, even if the outward expansion were very small compared to the inward expansion it has been calculated that this method gives very low efficiency: with 12 M_c an efficiency of only about 10^{-9} was calculated.

A better arrangement is the "boron bubble" scheme. B^{10} has the largest known absorption cross-section for fast neutrons, $1.52 \cdot 10^{-24} cm^2$. Suppose we take a large mass of active material and put in enough boron to make the mass just critical. The device is then fired by adding some more active material or tamper. As the reaction proceeds, the boron is compressed and is less effective at absorbing neutrons than when not compressed. This can be seen most readily if one considers the case in which the bubbles are large compared to the mean depth in which a neutron goes in boron before being absorbed. Then their effectiveness in removing neutrons will be proportional to their total area and so will drop on compression. Hence v' will increase as the bubbles are compressed. If the bomb is sufficiently large this tendency is bound to overweigh the opposing one due to the general expansion of the bomb material, since the distance the edge of the bomb must move to produce a given decrease in v' increases with the radius of the bomb, whereas for a larger bomb the distance the edge of a bubble must move is unchanged since it is not necessary to increase the radius of the bubbles but only to use more of them.

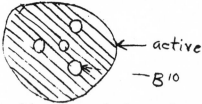

The density of particles (electrons plus nuclei) in boron is 8.3×10^{23} particle/cm^3 while in uranium it is more than 5 times greater. Therefore as soon as the reaction has proceeded to the point where there is a high degree of ionization and the material behaves as a gas, there will be a great action to compress the boron. An opposing tendency to the one desired will be the stirring or turbulence acting to mix the boron uniformly with the uranium but the time scale is too short for this to be effective.

It can be shown that if initially $v' = 0$, allowing for the boron absorption, and if no expansion of the outer edge occurs, then v' will rise to $v' \approx \frac{1}{4}(v-1)$ by compression of the boron. This scheme requires at least five times the critical mass for no boron, and the efficiency is low unless considerably more is used.

If one uses just that amount of boron which makes twice the no-boron critical mass be just critical, then the efficiency is lower by a factor of at least 30.

All autocatalytic schemes that have been thought of so far require large amounts of active material, are low in efficiency unless very large amounts are used, and are dangerous to handle. Some bright ideas are needed.

22. Conclusion

From the preceding outline we see that the immediate experimental program is largely concerned with measuring the neutron properties of various materials, and with the ordnance problem. It is also necessary to start new studies on techniques for direct experimental determination of critical size and time scale, working with large but sub-critical amounts of active material.

Endnotes

1. Imagine that we have a thin sheet of uranium foil of area A and thickness d. What does a neutron approaching the foil from a perpendicular direction see? It sees each uranium nucleus as a little circle of area σ (sigma, the Greek letter s), like this:

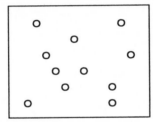

The formula for the area σ is σ = πR^2. This is the area the neutron has to hit, the geometrical cross section. If the nucleus has a radius R of 10^{-12} cm, then

$$\sigma = 3.14 \cdot (10^{-12})^2 \approx 3 \cdot 10^{-24} \qquad (1)$$

How densely populated with uranium atoms is our sheet of foil? The number of uranium atoms per cubic centimeter can be obtained from the number per gram times the number of grams of uranium there are in a cubic centimeter. The density of uranium metal is 19 grams/cc. Borrowing the figure for the number of uranium nuclei per gram from Section 2, we find that the number per cc of uranium is

$$n = 19 \cdot 2.58 \cdot 10^{21} = 4.9 \cdot 10^{22} \text{ nuclei/cc} \qquad (2)$$

The distance between uranium nuclei is

$$1/\sqrt[3]{n}$$

or

$$2.7 \cdot 10^{-8} \text{ cm} \tag{3}$$

The separation between nuclei is thus 27,000 times the radius of the nuclei. The foil is not densely populated; every neutron that bombards it isn't going to find a target.

The volume of the foil is the area times the thickness, A times d; thus the number of nuclei in the foil is:

$$nAd \tag{4}$$

The total area filled by these nuclei is just

$$nAd\sigma \tag{5}$$

A neutron passing at a random point through the foil has a chance, given by the total area of the nuclei divided by the total area of the foil, of hitting a nucleus. The probability, C, of a collision in passing through the foil is given by:

$$C = \frac{\text{area of nuclei}}{A} = n\sigma d \tag{6}$$

The probability of a neutron passing through the foil without a collision is then

$$1 - C = 1 - n\sigma d \tag{7}$$

This difference gives us a method of measuring the cross section. We need a source—an apparatus that will produce a nearly parallel beam of neutrons—and a detector—an instrument that will give a reading proportional to the number of neutrons that pass through it. We place the detector in the beam of neutrons and measure the number detected in a given period of time. Then we interpose the foil and read the number detected for the same period of time. That number will be less. The ratio of the reading with the foil in place to the reading without the foil gives us $1 - n\sigma d$, and since we know n and d, we can calculate σ.

We have assumed here that a collision removes a neutron from the beam, so that the detector doesn't count it. What if the collision results in a fission and two neutrons come out? There are other processes as well that lead to the emission of secondary neutrons. The distinguishing feature of secondary neutrons, however, is that they come out at a distribution of angles. The fact that they are moving in different directions makes it possible to distinguish them from the neutrons of the primary beam. If the detector is set sufficiently far from the foil, all the secondary neutrons will miss it, as shown in the following figure:

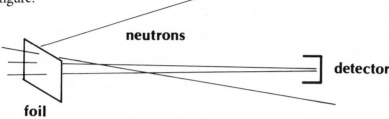

neutrons

detector

foil

If we write equation (6) in this form:

$$\frac{C}{d} = n\sigma$$

then the left-hand side is the number of collisions a neutron makes per centimeter in passing through uranium. The reciprocal of this is the number of centimeters per collision. It's called the mean free path—the distance a neutron traveling through uranium moves, on the average, before making a collision. At the beginning of this discussion, when we said that we used a thin foil, we meant that the thickness of the foil was small compared to the mean free path.

Not every collision in uranium produces a fission.

The fraction of the collisions that produce fission times the total cross section is called the fission cross section, denoted by σ_f. To measure the fission cross section we would need a different detector, one that can detect fission fragments and count the number of fissions. We would place the uranium within the detector and count the fissions. The number of counts is then $N\sigma_f d$ times the number of neutrons going through the detector. From this we can calculate the fission cross section.

2. To decide how a chain reaction is progressing in a sphere of uranium, we have to ask two questions: (1) How many neutrons are being produced per second in the sphere? (2) How many are escaping per second across the surface of the sphere? We approach this problem rather obliquely by asking the same questions about a small element of volume within the sphere: how many neutrons per second are being produced in the volume, and how many are escaping across its surface?

To answer the first question, go back to the discussion in endnote 1 about the number of collisions produced in a thin foil. The number of collisions a neutron makes in passing through the foil is $n\sigma d$, where n is the number of nuclei per cc, σ is the total cross section, and d is the thickness of the foil. The fraction of collisions that give a fission is σ_f/σ. The number of fissions in the foil is

$$C_f = n\sigma d \, \frac{\sigma_f}{\sigma} = n\sigma_f d \tag{1}$$

The neutrons have velocity v. The time it takes them to cross the foil is given by

$$d = vt \tag{2}$$

and the rate of producing fissions—the number of fissions per second—is simply

$$\frac{C_f}{t} = nv\sigma_f \tag{3}$$

The reciprocal of this number is the time per collision:

$$\tau = \frac{1}{n\sigma_f v} \tag{4}$$

and with this equation we can check the value given in the *Primer*. The velocity of a 1 Mev neutron is $1.4 \cdot 10^9$ cm/sec:

$$\tau = \frac{1}{4.9 \times 10^{22} \;\; 1.5 \times 10^{-24} \;\; 1.4 \times 10^9} = 10^{-8} \text{ sec} \tag{5}$$

In a fission, ν neutrons are produced and one is absorbed. So if there are N neutrons per cubic centimeter in our little volume, the net number of neutrons being produced per second per unit volume is

$$\frac{N(\nu - 1)}{\tau} \tag{6}$$

(Inelastic scattering in U^{235} doesn't come into the production rate, since it produces a neutron for every neutron absorbed. It comes in only indirectly in reducing the average velocity of the neutrons and thus affecting τ.)

The question of the number of neutrons lost across the surface of the volume is harder. So let's first consider a simpler model. Let's suppose that all the neutrons are moving with velocity v in the same direction, which can be either to the left or the right. We'll call this direction the x direction. That is, x measures the distance parallel to the neutrons' trajectories. We'll suppose that collisions take place which reverse the direction of the neutrons.

Now suppose that the density of neutrons is constant—that is, that the density doesn't depend on x. Such a system in stable equilibrium will have an equal number of neutrons moving to the left and to the right. If more neutrons started moving to the right, there would be more collisions changing direction from right to left than there would be from left to right, and so the distribution would rapidly equalize.

Let's call the neutron density N. Now consider a plane perpendicular to the direction of neutron motion—like a hall archway under which people pass walking left and right. We ask ourselves, how many neutrons per square centimeter per second cross this plane moving, let's say, to the right? That number would be

$$\tfrac{1}{2}Nv/cm^2/sec, \tag{7}$$

the factor $\tfrac{1}{2}$ because only half the neutrons are moving to the right. The number per cm^2/sec is called the neutron current. The current moving to the left will be exactly the same under equilibrium conditions, so the net number of neutrons crossing the plane will be zero.

Now suppose that the neutron density varies with the distance, as in figure 5:

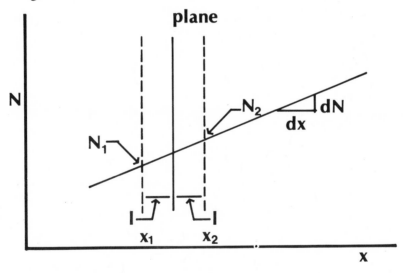

If the density changes by an amount dN in going a distance dx, then dN divided by dx is the change in N per centimeter:

$$\frac{dN}{dx} = \text{change in N/cm}$$

Now we observe that the neutrons crossing the plane from the left made their last collision, on the average, at a distance equal to the mean free path (designated 1 in the figure) to the left. The current to the right is therefore

$$\tfrac{1}{2} N_1 v$$

The current to the left is

$$\tfrac{1}{2} N_2 v$$

and the net current across the plane is

$$j = \tfrac{1}{2}(N_1 - N_2)v \qquad (8)$$

Now, $(N_2 - N_1)$ is equal to the rate of change of N per centimeter times the distance between x_1 and x_2, which is two times 1, the mean free path. So $(N_2 - N_1)$ is given by

$$N_2 - N_1 = \frac{dN}{dx} 21 \qquad (9)$$

Combining the last two equations gives us for the current

$$j = -lv \frac{dN}{dx} \qquad (10)$$

(By our convention a current to the left is a negative current and a current to the right a positive current. If the line sloped the other way, then dN/dx would be negative and the current would be positive, obviously the right answer.)

The difference when the neutrons move in *all* directions is that neutrons move not only in the direction towards the plane, but also in the two directions parallel to the plane (e.g., in our sketch, vertically and out of the plane of the paper). Motions parallel to the plane have no effect in carrying neutrons across the plane, so the current derived for our simplified, one-dimensional case has to be divided by three to get the right answer when the neutrons move in all directions. For this case, then, we have for the current

$$j = \frac{-lv}{3} \frac{dN}{dx} \qquad (11)$$

With this result in hand, we can return to our problem of the change in the number of neutrons in a small volume due to neutrons escaping through its surface. Consider a small volume of area A and thickness S:

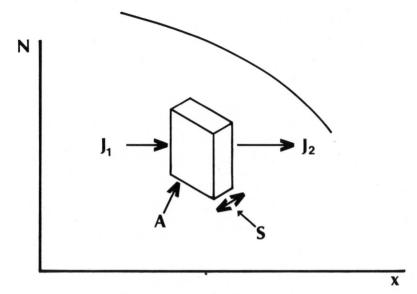

A current labeled J_1 crosses the left face of the volume, a current labeled J_2 the right face. The number of neutrons entering the volume from the left per second is just the current times the area of the surface, J_1A. The number of neutrons crossing the right face per second is J_2A. The net change per second, therefore, is the difference between the number leaving and the number entering:

$$\text{Loss of neutrons in volume/sec} = (J_2 - J_1)A \qquad (12)$$

If the curve of neutron density versus x is a straight line, as in figure 5, the currents J_1 and J_2 would be equal and there would be no net change in the number of neutrons in the volume. However, if the neutron density versus x is a curve, as in figure 6, the current depends on the position x. Since the curve gets steeper to the right, the current is bigger to the right than it is to the left. Therefore the current J_2 will be larger than the current J_1, and there will be a net loss of neutrons from the volume. The difference between J_2 and J_1 is the rate of change of J with x times the thickness S:

$$J_2 - J_1 = \frac{dJ}{dx} S \qquad (13)$$

Inserting this into equation (12) gives us

$$\text{Loss of neutrons in volume/sec} = \frac{dJ}{dx} AS \qquad (14)$$

Now, A times S is the volume of our region, so if we divide by the volume AS we get the loss of neutrons per second per unit volume:

$$\text{Loss of neutrons/cm}^3\text{/sec} = \frac{dJ}{dx} \tag{15}$$

Now we're prepared to write down our basic equation. In any little region in the gadget, the increase in the neutron density per second is just the net number of neutrons made by fission per second, minus the number escaping due to diffusion across the surface. This is the content of equation (16):

$$\frac{dN}{dt} = \frac{(\nu - 1)}{\tau} N - \frac{dJ}{dx} \tag{16}$$

Here t is the time, so the term on the left is the change in neutron density per second. The first term on the right is the net number of neutrons made by fission per second, as given by equation (6). The second term on the right is the loss of neutrons by diffusion, given by equation (15). We can combine equations (11) and (16) at the expense of introducing a new notation. The last term on the right in equation (16) can be written using equation (11), as

$$-\frac{dJ}{dx} = \frac{lv}{3} \frac{d(dN/dx)}{dx} \tag{17}$$

The last factor on the right is the rate of change of the rate of change of N with distance. Since it's rather awkward to write, it's customary to abbreviate it as

$$-\frac{dJ}{dx} = \frac{lv}{3} \frac{d^2N}{dx^2} \tag{18}$$

where the notation d^2N/dx^2 simply means the rate of change of the rate of change of N. For example, if we applied this notation to the motion of an automobile whose position is given by a distance S, then the velocity is the rate of change of distance with time, $v = dS/dt$, and the acceleration is the rate of change of velocity with time, which would be written

$$a = \frac{dv}{dt} = \frac{d^2S}{dt^2} \tag{19}$$

Inserting equation (18) into equation (16) we obtain the diffusion equation,

$$\frac{dN}{dt} = \frac{(\nu - 1)}{\tau} N + \frac{lv}{3} \frac{d^2N}{dx^2} \tag{20}$$

So far, we've been considering neutron densities varying in only one direction. We can easily generalize to the case where neutron density depends on all three direction coordinates, x, y, and z. In this case there will be neutron currents in all three directions, and the neutron loss from a small volume will be the sum of the losses in all three directions,

$$J_x = -\frac{lv}{3} \frac{dN}{dx}, \, J_y = -\frac{lv}{3} \frac{dN}{dy}, \, J_z = -\frac{lv}{3} \frac{dN}{dz}, \tag{21}$$

$$\frac{dN}{dt} = \frac{(\nu-1)}{\tau} N - \left(\frac{dJ_x}{dx} + \frac{dJ_y}{dy} + \frac{dJ_z}{dz} \right), \tag{22}$$

$$\frac{dN}{dt} = \frac{(\nu-1)}{\tau} N + \frac{lv}{3} \left(\frac{d^2N}{dx^2} + \frac{d^2N}{dy^2} + \frac{d^2N}{dz^2} \right). \tag{23}$$

Apart from notation, equation (22) is identical with the first equation in Section 10 of the *Primer*, N-dot being an abbreviation for dN/dt, and div *j* being an abbreviation for the last three terms in equation (22). Similarly, equation (23) is the same as the equation for N-dot in Section 10 near the top of page 26, delta N being an abbreviation for the three terms in the brackets in equation (23) and D equaling lv/3.

One point remains to be explained: the significance of transport mean free path and transport cross section. The *Primer* gives D as lv/3 with l the "transport mean free path," defined as l=1/nσ$_t$ with n the number of nuclei per cc and σ$_t$ the "transport cross section." In deriving equation (11) for the transport current, we implicitly assumed that the neutrons emerging from the collision were spherically symmetric—that is, went with equal probability in all directions. In fact, the elastically scattered neutrons are peaked in the forward direction—that is, in the direction in which the neutron that made the collision was moving before the collision. If the neutron is scattered through a very small angle, its subsequent path is almost the same as it would have been if there had been no scattering at all. Therefore, such a collision doesn't really affect the transport of neutrons and shouldn't be counted in calculating the mean free path. This effect is taken into account by introducing the transport cross section, in which the elastic scattering is multiplied by 1 minus the average cosine of the angle of scattering:

$$\text{Transport } \sigma_{el} = \sigma_{el} (1 - <\cos \theta>) \tag{24}$$

(The angular brackets mean: take the average value of the cosine.)

The cosine for forward scattering—for $\theta = 0$—equals 1; for 90 degree scattering 0; for 180 degree scattering -1. If the scattering is spherically symmetric, the average value of the cosine is zero, and there's no difference between the transport cross section and the cross section itself. On the other hand, if the scattering is peaked forward, the average cosine will be positive and the transport cross section will be smaller. These are the considerations the *Primer* uses to calculate the transport cross section. The l that appears in equation (23) should be the transport mean free path.

The solution of equation (23) is a straightforward mathematical problem. To complete the solution, however, we need, in addition to equation (23), a boundary condition—that is, a condition that identifies the outer edge of the sphere. In Section 10 of the *Primer* this is rather apologetically given as $N = 0$ at the boundary. We can easily derive a more reliable estimate. According to equation (7), the current at the boundary is $\frac{1}{2}Nv$. For consistency, this should equal the current given by equation (11). This gives us the condition

$$\frac{1}{2}Nv = -\frac{1}{3} \, lv \, \frac{dN}{dr} \tag{25}$$

(To conform to the geometry of the present problem, I've written dr rather than dx, r being the radial distance from the center of the sphere.)

So at the edge of the sphere, boundary $r = R$, we have the boundary condition given by

$$N = -\frac{2}{3} \, l \, \frac{dN}{dr} \tag{26}$$

If we use this boundary condition, we obtain, for the critical radius of an untamped sphere of 25, 9.26 cm—quite close to the value "about 9 cm" given by the more exact theory quoted in Section 10.

The critical radius depends on two numbers: the neutron excess— that is, the net number of neutrons produced per collision, which is given by

$$(\nu - 1)\sigma_f / \sigma_t \tag{27}$$

and the transport mean free path. And since the radius is proportional to the mean free path, which is inversely proportional to the density of material, the critical volume is proportional to $1/\text{density}^3$, while the critical mass, which is the density times the critical volume, is proportional to $1/\text{density}^2$. This is important in estimating the efficiency of the explosion, as mentioned earlier. With the boundary condition as indicated in equation (26), the dependence on the neutron excess is not as simple as indicated in the scaling law given at the end of Section 10.

It remains to explain the remarks in Section 10 about the limitations of elementary diffusion theory. In our derivation of equation (11), we used the fact there are currents $-+/-\tfrac{1}{2}Nv-$ across a plane perpendicular to the neutron gradient. However, the very fact that there is a net current shows that the currents across the plane are not quite equal. This isn't a serious discrepancy as long as the net current is small compared to $\tfrac{1}{2}Nv$:

$$\left|\frac{lv}{3}\frac{dN}{dx}\right| \ll \tfrac{1}{2}Nv$$

or

$$\left|\frac{1}{3}\frac{dN}{dx}\right| \ll \tfrac{1}{2}N \tag{28}$$

This is the limitation on elementary diffusion theory referred to in Section 10. The vertical bars mean the absolute value—that is, the quantity on the left is to be taken as positive. Note that the boundary condition, equation (26), cuts off the solution at the point where the two sides of equation (28) become equal. But quite aside from boundary conditions, it can be shown that equation (28) requires that in the active material the neutron excess, equation (27), be small compared to one. For uranium this number is $1.2 \cdot 1.5/4 = .45$, not at all small compared to one. One might therefore have doubts about the accuracy of the solution given by the elementary theory.

During the 1942 Berkeley summer preceding the opening of Los Alamos, I asked Eldred Nelson and Stan Frankel, two young members of the Berkeley theoretical group, to look back at the derivation of equation (11) and to try to improve it by correcting the left and right currents to take account of the net current across the surface. They did better than that. As I mentioned earlier, they discovered an exact solution of the problem that was not limited at all by condition (28). I remember their excitement and pleasure when they reported their findings. While the more exact theory gave an answer quite close to that found with the elementary diffusion theory, it allowed us to assert the accuracy of the results with considerably more certainty.

Appendix I

The Frisch-Peierls
Memorandum

Rudolf Peierls, a theoretical physicist and a German Jew, traveled to England in 1933 on a Rockefeller Fellowship. With the Nazi purge of the German universities that year he chose to stay in England (he became a naturalized citizen in 1940 and later was knighted for his work on atomic energy). Otto Frisch, a theoretical physicist and an Austrian Jew, emigrated to England from Germany in the summer of 1939. Both men were established at the University of Birmingham when the Second World War began. Because they were technically enemy aliens, they were excluded from the critical radar development work then proceeding at Birmingham under Mark Oliphant. They turned their attention to the question of whether nuclear fission could be applied to make an explosive. Peierls had derived and published a formula for determining critical mass; Frisch had looked into a process—gaseous thermal diffusion—for enriching uranium in the rare fissile isotope U^{235}. That work prepared them for the realizations that led to the historic memoranda reproduced below: that a relatively small quantity of purified U^{235} would be required to make an atomic bomb, and that such a quantity might be prepared in a matter of weeks once the necessary industrial-scale apparatus was built. They discussed their ideas with Oliphant, who encouraged them to write them down. Oliphant delivered their memoranda to the British government, which formed a committee to assess its military implications. In 1941 the M.A.U.D. committee's recommendations, communicated to President Franklin D. Roosevelt, catalyzed the decision to fund the Manhattan Project.

The first of the two Frisch-Peierls memoranda was lost to history until the British historian Ronald W. Clark discovered it among the papers of Henry Tizard, the influential British science administrator, some twenty years after the end of the war. It appears to have been intended for government and military officials who were not scientists; it offers a general overview of the possibilities, including an early statement of the theory of deterrence. The second memorandum is more detailed and technical. These documents reached Tizard's desk on 19 March 1940.

Memorandum on the Properties of a Radioactive 'Super-bomb'[1]

The attached detailed report concerns the possibility of constructing a 'super-bomb' which utilises the energy stored in atomic nuclei as a source of energy. The energy liberated in the explosion of such a super-bomb is about the same as that produced by the explosion of 1,000 tons of dynamite. This energy is liberated in a small volume, in which it will, for an instant, produce a temperature comparable to that in the interior of the sun. The blast from such an explosion would destroy life in a wide area. The size of this area is difficult to estimate, but it will probably cover the centre of a big city.

In addition, some part of the energy set free by the bomb goes to produce radioactive substances, and these will emit very powerful and dangerous radiations. The effects of these radiations is greatest immediately after the explosion, but it decays only gradually and even for days after the explosion any person entering the affected area will be killed.

Some of this radioactivity will be carried along with the wind and will spread the contamination; several miles downwind this may kill people.

In order to produce such a bomb it is necessary to treat a few cwt. of uranium by a process which will separate from the uranium its light isotope (U_{235}) of which it contains about 0.7%. Methods for the separation of such isotopes have recently been developed. They are slow and they have not until now been applied to uranium, whose chemical properties give rise to technical difficulties. But these diffi-

---

1. Reproduced from Ronald W. Clark, *Tizard* (MIT Press, 1965), 215–17.

culties are by no means insuperable. We have not sufficient experience with large-scale chemical plant to give a reliable estimate of the cost, but it is certainly not prohibitive.

It is a property of these super-bombs that there exists a 'critical size' of about one pound. A quantity of the separated uranium isotope that exceeds the critical amount is explosive; yet a quantity less than the critical amount is absolutely safe. The bomb would therefore be manufactured in two (or more) parts, each being less than the critical size, and in transport all danger of a premature explosion would be avoided if these parts were kept at a distance of a few inches from each other. The bomb would be provided with a mechanism that brings the two parts together when the bomb is intended to go off. Once the parts are joined to form a block which exceeds the critical amount, the effect of the penetrating radiation always present in the atmosphere will initiate the explosion within a second or so.

The mechanism which brings the parts of the bomb together must be arranged to work fairly rapidly because of the possibility of the bomb exploding when the critical conditions have just only been reached. In this case the explosion will be far less powerful. It is never possible to exclude this altogether, but one can easily ensure that only, say, one bomb out of 100 will fail in this way, and since in any case the explosion is strong enough to destroy the bomb itself, this point is not serious.

We do not feel competent to discuss the strategic value of such a bomb, but the following conclusions seem certain:

1. As a weapon, the super-bomb would be practically irresistible. There is no material or structure that could be expected to resist the force of the explosion. If one thinks of using the bomb for breaking through a line of fortifications, it should be kept in mind that the radioactive radiations will prevent anyone from approaching the affected territory for several days; they will equally prevent defenders from reoccupying the affected positions. The advantage would lie with the side which can determine most accurately just when it is safe to re-enter the area; this is likely to be the aggressor, who knows the location of the bomb in advance.

2. Owing to the spread of radioactive substances with the wind, the bomb could probably not be used without killing large numbers of civilians, and this may make it unsuitable as a weapon for use by this country. (Use as a depth charge near a naval base suggests itself, but

even there it is likely that it would cause great loss of civilian life by flooding and by the radioactive radiations.)

3. We have no information that the same idea has also occurred to other scientists but since all the theoretical data bearing on this problem are published, it is quite conceivable that Germany is, in fact, developing this weapon. Whether this is the case is difficult to find out, since the plant for the separation of isotopes need not be of such a size as to attract attention. Information that could be helpful in this respect would be data about the exploitation of the uranium mines under German control (mainly in Czechoslovakia) and about any recent German purchases of uranium abroad. It is likely that the plant would be controlled by Dr. K. Clusius (Professor of Physical Chemistry in Munich University), the inventor of the best method for separating isotopes, and therefore information as to his whereabouts and status might also give an important clue.

At the same time it is quite possible that nobody in Germany has yet realised that the separation of the uranium isotopes would make the construction of a super-bomb possible. Hence it is of extreme importance to keep this report secret since any rumour about the connection between uranium separation and a super-bomb may set a German scientist thinking along the right lines.

4. If one works on the assumption that Germany is, or will be, in the possession of this weapon, it must be realised that no shelters are available that would be effective and could be used on a large scale. The most effective reply would be a counter-threat with a similar bomb. Therefore it seems to us important to start production as soon and as rapidly as possible, even if it is not intended to use the bomb as a means of attack. Since the separation of the necessary amount of uranium is, in the most favourable circumstances, a matter of several months, it would obviously be too late to start production when such a bomb is known to be in the hands of Germany, and the matter seems, therefore, very urgent.

5. As a measure of precaution, it is important to have detection squads available in order to deal with the radioactive effects of such a bomb. Their task would be to approach the danger zone with measuring instruments, to determine the extent and probable duration of the danger and to prevent people from entering the danger zone. This is vital since the radiations kill instantly only in very strong doses whereas weaker doses produce delayed effects and hence near the

edges of the danger zone people would have no warning until it were too late.

For their own protection, the detection squads would enter the danger zone in motor-cars or aeroplanes which are armoured with lead plates, which absorb most of the dangerous radiation. The cabin would have to be hermetically sealed and oxygen carried in cylinders because of the danger from contaminated air.

The detection staff would have to know exactly the greatest dose of radiation to which a human being can be exposed safely for a short time. This safety limit is not at present known with sufficient accuracy and further biological research for this purpose is urgently required.

As regards the reliability of the conclusions outlined above, it may be said that they are not based on direct experiments, since nobody has ever yet built a super-bomb, but they are mostly based on facts which, by recent research in nuclear physics, have been very safely established. The only uncertainty concerns the critical size for the bomb. We are fairly confident that the critical size is roughly a pound or so, but for this estimate we have to rely on certain theoretical ideas which have not been positively confirmed. If the critical size were appreciably larger than we believe it to be, the technical difficulties in the way of constructing the bomb would be enhanced. The point can be definitely settled as soon as a small amount of uranium has been separated, and we think that in view of the importance of the matter immediate steps should be taken to reach at least this stage; meanwhile it is also possible to carry out certain experiments which, while they cannot settle the question with absolute finality, could, if their result were positive, give strong support to our conclusions.

On the Construction of a 'Super-bomb'; Based on a Nuclear Chain Reaction in Uranium

The possible construction of 'super-bombs' based on a nuclear chain reaction in uranium has been discussed a great deal and arguments have been brought forward which seemed to exclude this possibility. We wish here to point out and discuss a possibility which seems to have been overlooked in these earlier discussions.

Uranium consists essentially of two isotopes, ^{238}U (99.3%) and ^{235}U (0.7%). If a uranium nucleus is hit by a neutron, three processes are possible: (1) scattering, whereby the neutron changes direction and, if its energy is above about 0.1 MeV, loses energy; (2) capture, when the neutron is taken up by the nucleus; and (3) fission, i.e. the nucleus breaks up into two nuclei of comparable size, with the liberation of an energy of about 200 MeV.

The possibility of a chain reaction is given by the fact that neutrons are emitted in the fission and that the number of these neutrons per fission is greater than 1. The most probably value for this figure seems to be 2.3, from two independent determinations.

However, it has been shown that even in a large block of ordinary uranium no chain reaction would take place since too many neutrons would be slowed down by inelastic scattering into the energy region where they are strongly absorbed by ^{238}U.

Several people have tried to make chain reaction possible by mixing the uranium with water, which reduces the energy of the neutrons still further and thereby increases their efficiency again. It seems fairly certain, however, that even then it is impossible to sustain a chain reaction.

In any case, no arrangement containing hydrogen and based on the action of slow neutrons could act as an effective super-bomb, because the reaction would be too slow. The time required to slow down a neutron is about 10^{-5} sec and the average time lost before a neutron hits a uranium nucleus is even 10^{-4} sec. In the reaction, the number of neutrons would increase exponentially, like $e^{t/\tau}$ where τ would be at least 10^{10-4} sec. When the temperature reaches several thousand degrees the container of the bomb will break and within 10^{-4} sec the uranium would have expanded sufficiently to let the neutrons escape and so to stop the reaction. The energy liberated would, therefore, be only a few times the energy required to break the container, i.e., of the same order of magnitude as with ordinary high explosives.

Bohr has put forward strong arguments for the suggestion that the fission observed with slow neutrons is to be ascribed to the rare isotope ^{235}U, and that this isotope has, on the whole, a much greater fission probability than the common isotope ^{238}U. Effective methods for the separation of isotopes have been developed recently, of which the method of thermal diffusion is simple enough to permit separation on a fairly large scale.

This permits, in principle, the use of nearly pure ^{235}U in such a bomb, a possibility which apparently has not so far been seriously considered. We have discussed this possibility and come to the conclusion that a moderate amount of ^{235}U would indeed constitute an extremely efficient explosive.

The behavior of ^{235}U under bombardment with fast neutrons is not known experimentally, but from rather simple theoretical arguments it can be concluded that almost every collision produces fission and that neutrons of any energy are effective. Therefore it is not necessary to add hydrogen, and the reaction, depending on the action of fast neutrons, develops with very great rapidity so that a considerable part of the total energy is liberated before the reaction gets stopped on account of the expansion of the material.

The critical radius r_0—i.e. the radius of a sphere in which the surplus of neutrons created by the fission is just equal to the loss of neutrons by escape through the surface—is, for a material with a given composition, in a fixed ratio to the mean free path of the neutrons, and this in turn is inversely proportional to the density. It therefore pays to bring the material into the densest possible form, i.e. the metallic state, probably sintered or hammered. If we assume, for ^{235}U, no appreciable scattering, and 2.3 neutrons emitted per fission, then the critical radius is found to be 0.8 times the mean free path. In the metallic state (density 15), and assuming a fission cross-section of 10^{-23} cm^2, the mean free patch would be 2.6 cm and r_0 would be 2.1 cm, corresponding to a mass of 600 grams. A sphere of metallic ^{235}U of a radius greater than r_0 would be explosive, and one might think of about 1 kg as a suitable size for the bomb.

The speed of the reaction is easy to estimate. The neutrons emitted in the fission have velocities of about 10^9 cm/sec and they have to travel 2.6 cm before hitting a uranium nucleus. For a sphere well above the critical size the loss through neutron escape would be small, so we may assume that each neutron, after a life of 2.6×10^{-9} sec, produces fission, giving birth to two neutrons. In the expression $e^{t/\tau}$ for the increase of neutron density with time, τ would be about 4×10^{-9} sec, very much shorter than in the case of a chain reaction depending on slow neutrons.

If the reactions proceeds until most of the uranium is used up, temperatures of the order of 10^{10} degrees and pressures of about 10^{13} atmospheres are produced. It is difficult to predict accurately the behavior of matter under these extreme conditions, and the mathematical difficulties of the problem are considerable. By a rough calculation we get the following expression for the energy liberated before the mass expands so much that the reaction is interrupted:

$$E = 0.2M(r^2/\tau^2) \sqrt{(r/r_0)-1)} \tag{1}$$

(M, total mass of uranium; r, radius of sphere; r_0, critical radius; τ, time required for neutron density to multiply by a factor e). For a sphere of diameter 4.2 cm ($r = 2.1$ cm),[2] $M = 4700$ grams, $\tau = 4 \times 10^{-9}$ sec, we find $E = 4 \times 10^{22}$ ergs, which is about one-tenth of the total fission energy. For a radius of about 8 cm ($M = 32$ kg) the whole fission energy is liberated, according to formula (1). For small radii the efficiency falls off even faster than indicated by formula (1) because τ goes up as r approaches r^0. The energy liberated by a 5 kg bomb would be equivalent to that of several thousand tons of dynamite, while that of a 1 kg bomb, though about 500 times less, would still be formidable.

It is necessary that such a sphere should be made in two (or more) parts which are brought together first when the explosion is wanted. Once assembled, the bomb would explode within a second or less, since one neutron is sufficient to start the reaction and there are several neutrons passing through the bomb in every second, from the cosmic radiation. (Neutrons originating from the action of uranium alpha rays on light-element impurities would be negligible provided the uranium is reasonably pure.) A sphere with a radius of less than about 3 cm could be made up in two hemispheres, which are pulled together by springs and kept separated by a suitable structure which is removed at the desired moment. A larger sphere would have to be composed of more than two parts, if the parts, taken separately, are to be stable.

It is important that the assembling of the parts should be done as rapidly as possible, in order to minimize the chance of a reaction getting started at a moment when the critical conditions have only just been reached. If this happened, the reaction rate would be much slower and the energy liberation would be considerably reduced; it would, however, always be sufficient to destroy the bomb.

It may be well to emphasize that a sphere only slightly below the critical size is entirely safe and harmless. By experimenting with spheres of gradually increasing size and measuring the number of neutrons emerging from them under a known neutron bombardment, one

2. Something is wrong here. At $\rho = 15$ the radius of a 4,700 gram sphere would be r = 4.2 (not diameter = 4.2 cm.) [RS].

could accurately determine the critical size, without any danger of a premature explosion.

For the separation of the ^{235}U, the method of thermal diffusion, developed by Clusius and others, seems to be the only one which can cope with the large amounts required. A gaseous uranium compound, for example, uranium hexafluoride, is placed between two vertical surfaces which are kept at a different temperature. The light isotope tends to get more concentrated near the hot surface, where it is carried upwards by the convection current. Exchange with the current moving downwards along the cold surface produces a fractionating effect, and after some time a state of equilibrium is reached when the gas near the upper end contains markedly more of the light isotope than near the lower end.

For example, a system of two concentric tubes, of 2 mm separation and 3 cm diameter, 150 cm long, would produce a difference of about 40% in the concentration of the rare isotope between its ends, and about 1 gram per day could be drawn from the upper end without unduly upsetting the equilibrium.

In order to produce large amounts of highly concentrated ^{235}U, a great number of these separating units will have to be used, being arranged in parallel as well as in series. For a daily production of 100 grams of ^{235}U of 90% purity, we estimate that about 100,000 of these tubes would be required. This seems a large number, but it would undoubtedly be possible to design some kind of a system which would have the same effective area in a more compact and less expensive form.

In addition to the destructive effect of the explosion itself, the whole material of the bomb would be transformed into a highly radioactive state. The energy radiated by these active substances will amount to about 20% of the energy liberated in the explosion, and the radiations would be fatal to living beings even a long time after the explosion.

The fission of uranium results in the formation of a great number of active bodies with periods between, roughly speaking, a second and a year. The resulting radiation is found to decay in such a way that the intensity is about inversely proportional to the time. Even one day after the explosion the radiation will correspond to a power expenditure of the order of 1000 kW, or to the radiation of a hundred tons of radium.

Any estimates of the effects of this radiation on human beings must be rather uncertain because it is difficult to tell what will happen to the radioactive material after the explosion. Most of it will probably be blown into the air and carried away by the wind. This cloud of radioactive material will kill everybody within a strip estimated to be several miles long. If it rained the danger would be even worse because active material would be carried down to the ground and stick to it, and persons entering the contaminated area would be subjected to dangerous radiations even after days. If 1% of the active material sticks to the debris in the vicinity of the explosion and if the debris is spread over an area of, say, a square mile, any person entering this area would be in serious danger, even several days after the explosion.

In these estimates, the lethal dose of penetrating radiation was assumed to be 1,000 Roentgen; consultation of a medical specialist on X-ray treatment and perhaps further biological research may enable one to fix the danger limit more accurately. The main source of uncertainty is our lack of knowledge as to the behavior of materials in such a super-explosion, and an expert on high explosives may be able to clarify some of these problems.

Effective protection is hardly possible. Houses would offer protection only at the margins of the danger zone. Deep cellars or tunnels may be comparatively safe from the effects of radiation, provided air can be supplied from an uncontaminated area (some of the active substances would be noble gases which are not stopped by ordinary filters).

The irradiation is not felt until hours later when it may be too late. Therefore it would be very important to have an organization which determines the exact extent of the danger area, by means of ionization measurements, so that people can be warned from entering it.

O. R. FRISCH
R. PEIERLS

The University, Birmingham

Appendix II

Biographical Notes

Hans **Bethe**, theoretical physicist, born Strasburg, Germany, 1906, emigrated to the United States in 1935, where he taught physics at Cornell University. From 1943 to 1946 he directed the theoretical physics division at Los Alamos. He was awarded the Nobel Prize in Physics in 1967.

Raymond Birge, experimental physicist, born Brooklyn, New York, 1887, was chairman of the Department of Physics at the University of California at Berkeley from 1933 to 1955.

Felix Bloch, theoretical physicist, born Zürich, Switzerland, 1905, taught physics at Stanford University from 1934 to 1971. He did war research at Stanford, Los Alamos, and Harvard. He received the Nobel Prize in Physics in 1952.

Niels Bohr, theoretical physicist, born Copenhagen, Denmark, 1885, founded quantum physics. He received the Nobel Prize in Physics in 1922. During the war he served as an adviser at Los Alamos.

Gregory Breit, theoretical physicist, born Russia, 1899, was a research associate of the Department of Terrestrial Magnetism of the Carnegie Institution of Washington from 1929 to 1944. He preceded Robert Oppenheimer as coordinator of fast-neutron studies for the Manhattan Project.

James Chadwick, experimental physicist, born Bollington, Cheshire, England, 1891, discovered the neutron, for which he received the Nobel Prize in Physics in 1935. He headed the British delegation to Los Alamos.

Arthur Holly Compton, experimental physicist, born Wooster, Ohio, 1892, directed the Metallurgical Laboratory at the University of Chicago from 1942 to 1945, which developed the first nuclear reactors and devised the chemical technology necessary to separate plutonium from uranium. He received the Nobel Prize in Physics in 1927.

Edward Condon, theoretical physicist, born Alamogordo, New Mexico, 1902, was associate professor of physics at Princeton University from 1930 to 1937 and director of the National Bureau of Standards from 1945 to 1951. He was associate director at Los Alamos in the first months of the laboratory's existence but resigned in a dispute over secrecy.

Paul Dirac, theoretical physicist, born Bristol, England, 1902, received the Nobel Prize in Physics in 1933. He was Lucasian professor of mathematics at Cambridge University from 1932 to 1969.

Enrico Fermi, experimental and theoretical physicist, born Rome, Italy, 1901, was the coinventor with Leo Szilard of the nuclear reactor and directed the building of the first such reactor at the Metallurgical Laboratory of the University of Chicago during the war, work culminating in December 1942 in the first manmade nuclear chain reaction. He received the Nobel Prize in Physics in 1938.

Richard Feynman, theoretical physicist, born New York City, 1918, worked in the theoretical division at Los Alamos. He received the Nobel Prize in Physics in 1965.

Stanley Frankel, theoretical physicist, born Los Angeles, California, 1919, worked at the Lawrence Radiation Laboratory and at Los Alamos.

Otto Robert Frisch, theoretical physicist, born Vienna, Austria, 1904, with his aunt Lise Meitner defined and named nuclear fission. His report on the possibility of a "super-bomb" catalyzed British investigation into the application of nuclear fission to war.

Maurice Goldhaber, theoretical physicist, born Lemberg, Austria, 1911, emigrated to the United States from England in 1938 and taught physics at the University of Illinois until 1973.

Leslie Richard Groves, U.S. Army engineer, born Albany, New York, 1896, built the Pentagon and directed the Manhattan Project.

Otto Hahn, radiochemist, born Frankfurt-am-Main, Germany, 1879, was the codiscoverer with Fritz Strassmann of nuclear fission, work for which the two men shared the Nobel Prize in Chemistry in 1944.

Werner Heisenberg, theoretical physicist, born Wurzburg, Germany, 1901, developed quantum mechanics, for which he won the Nobel Prize in Physics in 1932. He worked on atomic-bomb and nuclear-reactor development in Germany during the war.

Frederic Joliot, experimental physicist, born Paris, France, 1900, was the codiscoverer with his wife Irene Curie of artificial radioactivity, work for which the Joliot-Curies received the Nobel Prize in Chemistry in 1935. With Hans von Halban and Leo Kowarski he first demonstrated secondary neutrons from fission in Paris in 1939.

Emil Konopinski, theoretical physicist, born Michigan City, Indiana, 1911, worked at Los Alamos from 1943 to 1946.

Charles Lauritsen, experimental physicist, born Holstebro, Denmark, 1892, taught at the California Institute of Technology from 1930 to 1962.

Ernest Lawrence, experimental physicist, born Canton, South Dakota, 1901, invented the cyclotron, work for which he received the Nobel Prize in Physics in 1939. He directed the electromagnetic separation of uranium at Berkeley and Oak Ridge during the war.

Edwin McMillan, experimental physicist, born Redondo Beach, California, 1907, was the discoverer of neptunium and the codiscoverer with Glenn Seaborg of plutonium, for which he received the Nobel Prize for Chemistry in 1951.

John Manley, experimental physicist, born Harvard, Illinois, 1907, was a scientist at Los Alamos during the war and subsequently associate director there.

Lise Meitner, theoretical physicist, born Vienna, Austria, 1878, developed the first theoretical understanding of nuclear fission with her nephew Otto Robert Frisch.

Eldred Nelson, theoretical physicist, born Starbuck, Minnesota, 1917, was a group leader in the theoretical physics division at Los Alamos during the war.

Kenneth Nichols, U.S. Army engineer, born Cleveland, Ohio, 1907, was second in command of the Manhattan Project.

Robert Oppenheimer, theoretical physicist, born New York City, 1904, founded and directed the Los Alamos Laboratory from 1943 to 1945.

Wolfgang Pauli, theoretical physicist, born Vienna, Austria, 1900, received the Nobel Prize in Physics in 1945.

I. I. Rabi, experimental physicist, born Rymanow, Austria, 1898, emigrated to the United States as a small child. From 1942 to 1945 he was associate director of the Radiation Laboratory at MIT, which developed radar, and a consultant at Los Alamos. He received the Nobel Prize in Physics in 1944.

Glenn Seaborg, nuclear chemist, born Ishpeming, Michigan, 1912, was the codiscoverer with Edwin Mcmillian of plutonium, for which he received the Nobel Prize for Chemistry in 1951. He developed the process for chemically separating plutonium from uranium that was applied at Hanford, Washington, to accumulate the plutonium for the Trinity and Nagasaki atomic bombs.

Emilio Segré, experimental physicist, born Rome, Italy, 1905, emigrated to the United States in 1938 and was a group leader at Los Alamos during the war. He won the Nobel Prize in Physics in 1959.

Fritz Strassmann, inorganic chemist, born Boppard, Germany, 1902, was the codiscoverer with Otto Hahn of nuclear fission, work for which the two men shared the Nobel Prize in Chemistry in 1944.

Edward Teller, theoretical physicist, born Budapest, Hungary, 1908, emigrated to the United States in 1935. He worked on the atomic and hydrogen bombs at Los Alamos during the war and in 1951 was the coinventor with the Polish mathematician Stanislaw Ulam of the U.S. hydrogen bomb.

Richard Tolman, theoretical physicist, born West Newton, Massachusetts, 1881, was dean of the graduate school of the California Institute of Technology from 1922 until his death in 1948.

John Van Vleck, theoretical physicist, born Middletown, Connecticut, 1899, was professor of physics at Harvard University from 1935 to 1969.

Eugene Wigner, theoretical physicist, born Budapest, Hungary, 1902, emigrated to the United States in 1930 and was professor of physics at Princeton University from 1938 to 1971. At the Metallurgical Laboratory of the University of Chicago during the war he designed the nuclear reactors built at Hanford, Washington, that produced plutonium for the first atomic bombs. He received the Nobel Prize in Physics in 1963.

John Williams, experimental physicist, born Asbestos Mines, Canada, 1908, was a research scientist at Los Alamos from 1943 to 1946.

Robert Wilson, experimental physicist, born Frontier, Wyoming, 1914, led the cyclotron group at Los Alamos from 1943 to 1944 and directed the experimental research division from 1944 to 1946.

Index